Zebra Finch

Zebra Finches as pets

Zebra Finches Keeping, Care, Pros and Cons,
Housing, Diet and Health.

by

Roger Rodendale

Table of Contents

Introduction

If you are planning to bring a bird home, you may want to look for all the options that are available to you. Now, many people will think twice about the option of buying a bird because they are told stories about how attention seeking birds like Macaws and Cockatoos can be. These birds make amazing pets but are extremely demanding on the owners when it comes to spending a lot of time with them. These birds can also get extremely dependent on their owners.

Most birds also need the most exotic toys and mental stimulation equipment that can be really expensive. Now, if you are looking for birds that are friendly and fun but low maintenance at the same time, then the Zebra Finch is the best possible option. It is likely that you have seen this little stout bird at popular pet stores.

Zebra Finches are among the most popular pet birds that are also readily available. Since these birds are prolific breeders, there are several individuals who breed these birds and sell them, too. So, if you are looking for a no fuss pet, the Zebra Finch may be your best option.

Of course, they have a care routine that is different from the other birds. What you need to know about Zebra Finches as the owner is how you can keep your bird healthy and happy. Although they are not as demanding and attention seeking as birds like the parrots, it does not mean that you can just leave some food in the bowl and expect your bird to take care of himself.

Like any other pet, when you bring a Zebra Finch home, you will have to understand the responsibility. Like any other bird, zebra Finches are also intelligent and sensitive creatures. You need to make sure that you understand the natural personality of these birds and do everything you can to retain that.

For instance, the Zebra Finch is very social and loves to interact. So, if you do not have any time to spend with your bird, you can bring home groups or pairs. They like to interact with their owners and members of their flock. You will be surprised at how responsive these creatures are. It almost feels like you can have long conversations with your pet once you are aware of their body language and vocalizations.

With this book, you will learn everything about the Zebra Finch from the feeding requirements, tips to keep them active and physically fit, breeding these birds, the common health problems that they may face and a lot more.

It is the perfect guide to Zebra Finches that is based entirely on the views of individuals who have a lot of experience with these birds. Thus, all the tips have been tried and tested and will make sure that your bird gets nothing short of the best.

This book has been composed with the idea of making your journey with your Zebra Finch as delightful as possible.

Chapter 1: About the Zebra Finch

The Zebra Finch is also popularly known as the Australian Finch. Of course, this bird is not the only Australian Finch as there are several other varieties that are available. However, since these birds are the most commonly found Australian Finch, the two names are usually considered synonyms.

These birds are domesticated widely and are known for their interesting personalities. Since these birds readily breed in captivity, mutations are very common. The more combinations of colors, the more attractive they become to the general public. In this chapter you will learn all about Zebra Finches, the general appearance, origins and the various mutations of these birds.

1. Basic appearance

Zebra Finches are often identified by their basic appearance that is more commonly known across the world. The male bird has grey colored wings and upper body parts. The belly of the bird is white in color. The contrasting red-orange legs and beak, make Zebra Finches quite exquisite.

The head has a cheek patch on either side. The typical tear drop marking under the eye of the bird is the best way to identify them. This usually ranges from fawn, brown, tan to orange in color. The sides of the bird or the flanks have a chestnut colored patch. This patch is covered with white dots.

The name Zebra Finch comes from the black and white stripes on the chest of the bird. These birds are magnificently colored and will just take your breath away.

Now, the females aren't entirely different from the male. They also have the white belly and grey wings. The beak and legs are a duller shade of orange and seem to be lighter.

The tear drop mark under the eye is almost always black in color for the female. The biggest difference between the male and the female lies in the chest striping and the cheek patches. The colors are absent and these areas are usually grey in color for the females. As for the juvenile birds, the coloring is almost like the females, with the exception of the beak being black in color. By the time the chicks are 90 days old, they develop all the colors of the adult Zebra Finch.

Breeding practices of the Zebra Finch have led to several mutations. As a result, you will see that the colors are entirely different and quite mixed up as well. Breeders have a lot of knowledge about genetics and its techniques that makes it possible to have so many mutations.

a. Types of genes
There are three types of genes that lead to all the mutations. The combinations of these genes vary to make different resultant colors and structures of the body. The three types of genes are:

- Dominant: If one parent of the finch has this dominant color then the offspring will display it too. In case of these dominant genes, zebras do not show any split traits. They will either carry the color or they won't. There are a few dominant mutations like black face, dominant silver, grey cheek, crested and fawn cheek.

  If the breeder wants to produce these dominant traits in the offspring, it is not necessary that both parents have the dominant mutation. If one parent is the normal basic grey variety and the other is of a dominant strain, it is almost guaranteed that the offspring will have the desired color. Usually half of the clutch will have the color that you are trying to get and the other half will have another color. Only the grey birds require both the parents to be of a dominant strain.

- **Recessive:** You will be able to see these color traits in the offspring only if both the parents have carried and showed these colors. The thing with recessive colors is that they tend to pop up when you do not really expect them to.

In many families of birds these traits are hidden for years. Only when you have the right pairing do these colors actually show. For instance, if two birds with the same recessive genes are bred, the offspring is likely to show them too. Of course, the birds who do not show these traits will be carriers of this trait. The most common recessive colors include pied, isabel. black breast, black cheek, orange breast, recessive silver, penguin and white.

- **Sex linked:** This is the easiest to understand, by the name. It is related to the sex of the bird. Usually these genes are seen on the X chromosome of the female. If the female has this gene, then it will be seen. In the case of males, the presence of this gene does not guarantee that they will show it. They may just be carriers of the gene.

Only when both parents of the male have this gene will he show it. The most common sex linked genes include chestnut, flanked white, fawn and light black.

The beauty of these birds is that there are several genes that work to make the beautiful colors on the body of these birds. One bird may carry several mutations and display several others. For example, it is possible to have a black face silver pied variety, which is the split between black cheek and yellow beak. In order to bring out the hidden genes, it is necessary to mate the bird with a female who is also a silver pied, recessive variety.

It is just impossible to say how many mutations of the birds exist today. There are new ones that are noticed from time to time. One of the most recent mutations has been named the George and several breeders are working on this color pattern. However, a few mutations have been recognized for show and exhibitions.

The next section will tell you in detail about all these color mutations. This will also help you recognize a Zebra Finch even if you are not dealing with a breeder who works with the original wild variety.

b. Recognized color mutations

Below is a list of color mutations that are widely known and recognized:

- **Original grey**: These birds are normally dark grey in color but may be available in several shades. They have orange cheeks and may have spotted flanks with brown marking. The zebra striped throat and the black breast are the most prominent feature. There are no extra colorations on the females.

- **Black breast**: This is one of the most popular of all the mutations. The males tend to have a large bar on the breast that is black in color along with a black cheek patch. This patch extends till the back of the head. The flanks have elongated and reddish white dots. Both genders do not have the typical tear shaped mark that you find just below the eye.

- **Black cheek:** This variety has a very usual appearance that makes it an interesting choice for most people. You will see the exact black patches on the cheek in both genders. The flanking is black with white spots in case of the male. Of course, it could also be brown in some cases.

- **Black face:** In case of these birds the whole face is black in color. This is the area between the eye and the beak of the bird. Even the breast and the underparts of the bird are black in color. Flanking may vary from red to brown with a few white dots. In case of the females, black coloration on the face is not as intense as it is on the male. They may have silver or gray facial area. These birds have a gorgeous contrasting yellow beak that makes them delightful to look at.

- **Chestnut flanked or marked white:** Both the male and the female tend to have body color that varies from ivory to white. The males tend to have normal cheek patches, breast bars and flanks. These markings are, however, not as strong as the ones you see on the greys. Females are fully white with just a white tear drop mark under the eye.

- **Crested:** These birds have feathers on the center top of their head. You will see this in both the genders. Some may have a full crest while in some birds you may only see a semi-circle. In some of the birds the feathers stand up like spikes and are completely straight.

- **Dominant silver:** In these birds the body color ranges from a shade of blue to silver grey. They are very similar to the recessive silver mutation but they tend to have cream or white flanking and cheeks. There is no trace of orange in these birds. They are also darker than the recessive silver birds.

- **Fawn:** These unique birds have tan or cinnamon brown colored body feathers in both males and females. In the case of the males, you will see the typical colorations. These birds are very easily available in pet stores because they are very common. Since this coloration is due to a sex linked gene, you will mostly find females in this color.

- **Fawn and grey cheek:** These birds are close to Florida Fancies in appearance. However, the breast bar and the tear drop marks are darker in case of these birds. Cheek color will vary from orange to grey with a possibility of fawn. The body color varies from cream to white. The several colors on the male's body make this mutation extremely beautiful. It is said, however, that you must not mate grey cheeks and fawn cheeks as the traits are dominant.

- **Florida fancy:** This mutation is also called the Isabel. The birds range from white to a slight cream color. The underparts have a very typical buff color. The full colors in the flanks and the cheeks are retained in case of the males. There are no breast bars in these birds. They do not have any traces of black either. The females look fully white in color and can be slightly cream in color. In case of the females, as well, there are no black markings. These birds are easy to recognize, as they do not have the typical tear marking.

- **Light back:** In case of these birds, the upper body coloration is very diluted. All the other areas including the breast, vent and underparts are white in color. The tail coverts have white markings in both genders. You can see bright cream patches on the cheek and flanks of the males. There are black markings on the tail and the breast bar that are dark and distinct.

- **Orange breast:** These birds are quite easy to spot. In case of the Orange breast birds, all the black markings are orange in color. You will also find a few specimens that may have a few specks of the black coloration on the body. The hens or females are very normal in appearance, except for the orange bars in the tail covert.

- **Penguin:** This mutation is rather fascinating and these birds are often confused with the pied variety. The upper body of the bird is dark and has silver or white markings. This coloration is seen in both males and females. The underparts and the upper part of the breast are bright white in color. The male birds do not have any markings on the breast. The cheeks and the flanks in the males are colored normally and may be a little diluted. In case of the females, the white cheek area is the most striking feature besides the underparts and the bright breast region. They do not have the typical tear mark, however.

- **Pied:** With the pied mutation, the best part is that you will never find two birds that look the same. Pied means that color like fawn and grey have patches of white in between. This mutation can be seen in almost any type of coloration. However, when it occurs with dark colors it looks extremely striking. In fact, white birds can also be pied but it is not seen obviously.

- **Recessive Silver:** These birds are a lighter version of the silver grey color. In case of the males, the orange coloration in the flanks and the cheeks are retained fully. The females lack any type of special coloration except for the silver grey coloration.

- **White:** A solid white bird is what you get with this coloration. The beak coloration allows you to distinguish between the male and the females. The females have beaks that are pale orange in color while the males have red beaks. In some cases, you will see silver or light grey dots that are called pearling. This is an indication that your bird is pied.

- **Yellow beak:** This is the oldest variety and both the genders have beaks that are dull yellow in color. This mutation is a lot more attractive when it occurs on the darker colored birds.

There are several speculations that albino varieties of Zebra Finches are available. This is not true although there are possibilities of albinos occurring in just about any animal or bird species. However, no breeder has produced a Zebra Finch that has been proved to be an albino.

In case of albinos, none of the color pigments are available. In such mutations, the birds would be fully white in color and the eyes would be pink or white in color. The beaks would be pale and the legs would have a pale appearance too.

Many individuals have claimed to have bred albino birds. However, most often, they are only producing white birds with yellow beaks. Other mutations include birds with red eyes. These varieties are seen in the USA but are more common in Australia and Europe.

The red coloration is just a trait but is not considered to be related to any albinism in Zebra Finches. Although all the above mentioned colors look entirely different from one another, they belong to the same species. This means that they can be bred together to create several other mutations.

As a result, there have been recent colorations such as the Pheao which is a combination of Florida fancy and the Black breast. They are white and orange in color. They may even have orange facial feathers that makes them look extremely fascinating. There are variations of the orange colorations when such combinations are tried out by breeders.

The above mentioned colors are the most common ones. Some of them are accepted for showing and exhibiting. The beauty of Zebra Finches is that the naturally occurring bird has so many colors that it is easy for mutations to happen. This in turn gives bird enthusiasts a lot of variety to choose from.

It is the possibility of getting new strains and colorations that also makes the birds so popular among breeders. There are several breeders across the world who are constantly working with these birds to help understand the possibilities in terms of mutations and colorations along with proper care options for the birds.

2. Range and Habitat

These birds are native to Australia and are found almost all over the continent. These birds are extremely social and will be seen living in flocks in their natural range. They may live either with other Zebra Finches or may even make flocks with other smaller birds.

In Australia, Zebra Finches tend to inhabit all the areas except for the coastal districts in the west, the south east and the south west as well as the northern regions of Kimberley. They are also seen in the Lesser Sunda Islands that are found in the north western part of Australia. They are the most widely found Finches in this region.

One interesting thing about Zebra Finches is that the flocks travel quite a bit. In case they experience any unfavorable conditions within the arid region that they live in, they will move to another area to look for their food and other requirements. These birds are very quick to abandon their nesting areas to look for new spots.

Zebra Finches also occur in the tropical and subtropical regions of Australasia, Africa and South East Asia. The nests that they build are used to roost when they are still not in the breeding season. This is one of the main reasons why the bird is also able to survive in areas of the world where temperatures can drop immensely at night. They may make roosting nests separately or may simply make use of the breeding nests that were made in the previous season for roosting.

These birds are extremely adaptable because of their behavior that takes them to several areas in search of food and shelter. This is why they are highly resistant to most diseases that commonly affect birds. They can live with very little water and food or may even eat large quantities. These birds will do decently well in smaller housing areas although it is recommended that you take perfect care about housing your Finches. They are also able to survive in the most extremes of temperatures. This is why you will find a Zebra Finch in the arid regions of Australia as well as the tropical regions of Asia.

Zebra Finches will inhabit several kinds of forests and grasslands. You will usually find these birds near a water source of some sort. They are found is steppe regions that have several trees and bushes. These areas are drier in comparison. In the continent of Australia, these birds are seen in the areas that are arid. They will inhabit wooded areas that are dry for most part of the year.

These birds are also found in towns and some cities and have grown immune to human activities and can actually survive quite peacefully despite human disturbances.

In the wild, they also have extremely adaptable nesting habits and are usually found nesting in low trees, bushes, on the ground, in rabbit holes, cracks and crevices, ledges and also nests that other birds build.

3. Taxonomy

The Zebra Finch belongs to the family of birds called Weaver Finches that are quite prevalent in Australia. Those birds are categorized under the family Estrildidae, that even the Zebra Finches belong to. The Zebra Finch was formerly known by the scientific name *Poephila guttata.* Today, the accepted name for these birds is *Taeniopygia guttata.* The aboriginal names for these birds are Nyeen-ka and Nyi Nyi.

These birds are natively found in Australia, Indonesia and East Timor. They have been, however, introduced to other parts of the world including the United States, Puerto Rico, Brazil and Portugal. Based on the natural occurrence, these birds have also been classified into two subspecies:

- *Taeniopygia guttata castanotis,* which is the sub species found all over Australia. This race is also divided further into the Chestnut-eared Finch or the *Taeniopygia castanotis.*
- *Taeniopygia guttatta guttatta* is seen in the lesser Sunda Islands, Sermata, Indonesia and Lombok along with the coastal regions of Australia.

These birds also have a very marked morphological difference. For example, the *T.g.guttatta* birds are a lot smaller than the *T.g.castanotis* birds. In addition to that the male birds from the former subspecies lack any barring near the upper breast and throat. The latter do possess breast bands that are small but very noticeable.

Commonly breeders have developed several names for these birds, in addition to ones that are quite misleading. Breeders in the United States will refer to these birds as "German" and "English" Finches. Of course, this has nothing to do with the country of origin of these birds and is merely a way of classifying the bird as per the size. You must not be confused about these birds being a different species either.

Finches were bred in Europe mainly for shows and competitions. The breeders in the European countries experimented with the size and shape of the birds tremendously. This resulted in some birds being stocky and others being longer. Now, the German Finches are birds that are cobby in their appearance. Basically, the body is rounded.

The American Fiches are the least altered variety and you will notice that these birds are closest in appearance to the wild species. Though these birds were originally imported from the countries that they have been named after, they are not a different variety of the Finches. Of course, when these birds are bred, they give rise to offspring of different sizes entirely.

4. Importance of Finches
Zebra Finches are known as the white lab rats of the Finch world. These birds have been highly experimented upon to give rise to

several mutations that are of great economic value. This has also given rise to several shows and competitions that provide a great scope for individuals who want to breed these birds on a professional level.

Several studies have been conducted on Zebra Finches not only to determine their behavior but also the behavior of other birds.

One of the most important traits of this species is the singing ability of the male birds. These are among the only birds that are known to sing very complex songs that are unlike any other birds that are known to us. They use vocalizations like 'oi's', 'a-has' and beeps.

Research has shown that the male offspring is able to learn the song that his father sings to the exact notes and tones. He will then make a few adjustments later on to develop a song of his own. These changes occur only as long as the bird is a juvenile. As soon as he reaches adulthood, he will never change his voice.

This vocalization ability of the Zebra Finch is of great importance to scientists and researchers. The learned behavior has made this bird a model avian for several organizations to investigate activities like learning, sensorimotor integrations and memory.

In fact, this bird plays a crucial role in the genome project. After the successful sequencing of the genome of the chicken, the Zebra Finch was the second bird whose genome was used in this project.

The human race is quite grand, no doubt. But it is birds like the Zebra Finch that could be the missing links in evolution. In fact the genome project has proven how important a bird as small as the Zebra Finch actually is. Not only are we able to learn about the species that the Zebra Finch belongs to but we are also able to compare the development process of these birds with all the other avian species. In fact, this bird can be considered a representation of a whole class of animals for this reason.

In the wild, the major role of these birds is that of seed dispensers. As they migrate long distances, they are also able to transport seeds across large distances to give rise to new plants and trees.

Chapter 2: Bringing the Bird Home

In places where Zebra Finches are common, people may even pick wild birds and rear them as their own. Of course, that is only possible when you have enough experience to help a wild bird or an injured bird cope with a whole new environment.

Although Zebra Finches are very easy to keep as birds, the source that you bring your bird home from makes all the difference. No doubt, these are the perfect first time bird owners' dream come true. But if you bring home a bird that is in poor condition, you may find it quite challenging to take care of the bird and ensure that all his or her requirements are met.

There are various options available to you if you want to bring home your first Zebra Finch.

1. Where to buy a finch

There are various options for you to source your first Zebra Finch from. The choice you make depends upon the variety of the bird that you are looking for in terms of color mutations. The good news is that Finches are relatively easy to acquire, as they are common household pets in most parts of the world. They are also cheaper options for bird lovers with birds costing anything between $12-$50 or £5-£25 per bird.

The different sources available are:

a. From a pet store

This is, perhaps, the easiest option for you, as most pet stores will have these birds up for sale. Since these birds are cheaper options, they are readily available at most stores.

The only limitation that you will find with a pet store is the variety of birds available. You may not find many color mutations besides white, silver, grey and chestnut flanked birds. As we saw in the previous chapter, there are close to 20 color mutations available and if you are looking for something specific, it is best that you get your bird from a breeder.

When you are buying from a pet store, the health of the bird should be your primary concern. Most often, the birds are kept in poor conditions and may not be healthy enough. Observing the bird is the best way to say if he is healthy or not. Here are a few signs that you should consider a warning signal:

- Puffy appearance
- Staying alone in a corner
- The bird looks injured
- The bird does not become alert when you approach it

You will also find that in some cases, feathers are missing from the body of the bird. This is usually a result of having too many birds crammed up in one small cage. This leads to confrontations between males, causing severe injuries in most cases.

If you notice too many feathers missing, you may want to pass on to the next bird. However, if it is only a few feathers, then you can buy the birds that catch your attention as the feathers are likely to grow back with proper care and nutrition. Only when you see that the skin has been damaged due to feather picking or feather loss should you be concerned about the birds' health.

If this is your first time buying Finches, you can look for assistance from a previous owner of even a recommended aviculturist who will help you pick out the healthiest birds.

When you are buying from a pet store, make sure that you know which one is male and which one is female if you are purchasing pairs. When you buy from a store, you can never be sure about the birds that are related and the ones that are not.

This is important if you plan to breed the birds and are looking for specific color mutations. It is then recommended that you get a male from one store and a female from the other store.

You see, when you decide to breed these birds, it is crucial that you get specimens that are not related to one another. That way, you can breed them with more chances of getting the right coloration for the offspring.

b. Buying from a breeder

Breeding Zebra Finches is quite a common practice. Since these birds breed readily and have a lot of interesting color mutations, there are several individuals who have taken to breeding these birds as a profession.

You can buy from a breeder if you are looking for specific color mutations or are looking at buying a bird for exhibition and show purposes. These birds are almost of the same cost even with breeders because of the ready breeding in captivity.

Most often, breeders will find it hard to sell off all the offspring that emerge in each breeding season and may give the birds away for lower prices than pet stores as well. Now, when you are looking at acquiring your bird from a breeder, you have two options:

- **Buying from an amateur breeder:** These are the individuals who normally breed the birds in their backyard as a hobby. They will not have several pairs and will only give away the surplus offspring in each breeding season. They are the best sources to get your Finches from as they really care about who takes the bird home.

   The disadvantage with hobby breeders is that they do not know about the best breeding practices in some cases. Therefore, the birds that are produced may be weak and ailing. It is best that you do not bring these birds home if you are a novice yourself. Not only will your current bird be extremely weak, the coming generations, if any, will only get weaker and unhealthier with time.

- **Show bird breeders:** These are the professionals who have spent a lot of time researching about Finches and will ensure that the offspring meet all the standards of show and exhibitions.

   These breeders only give away those birds which do not entirely meet the standards of showing. The best birds are reserved for exhibitors or for the breeder himself.

If you are looking for birds to keep as pets, you may not have much to worry about in terms of the high standards. However, you can be sure that any bird you pick will be strong and healthy in most cases.

The disadvantage with these breeders is the possibility of hereditary defects that are the result of experimentation to get the right color mutation with each bird. Many ornithologists and bird enthusiasts encourage the purchase of Finches that are of the original wild variety. They believe that this is the only way to preserve the birds as they are seen in nature.

c. Buying online

If you type the words "Buy Zebra Finches" on any popular search engine, you will see a list of websites that will sell these birds online, including e-commerce giants like Ebay.

You must avoid buying birds online as much as possible. If you are purchasing from a breeder that you are familiar with, you may look at placing an order on his website. However, if you are looking at websites of complete strangers, it is best that you do not buy from them unless you can actually visit the facility once.

You see, getting birds shipped means that you can never be entirely sure about the standards of the bird that you are going to get. If you get a sick bird home, chances are that you will not be able to take good care. If you send the bird back, it is most certainly going to die before it goes back to where it came from.

d. Adopting a bird

If you live in an area where these birds are commonly found in the wild, you are sure to have several encounters with them. Sometimes, you may chance upon a bird that is unwell or has been hurt. You certainly have the option of taking this bird under your care and giving him a good life.

However, this is a good idea only if you know about caring for birds that are not in the best physical condition. It requires a lot of time and effort and the birds may also have a lot of behavioral issues that you need to deal with, as well.

"Rehoming" Finches is a very popular concept too. There are various forums online where you can find owners who want to give their birds a new home. This is probably because they are relocating or are unable to provide necessary care for their birds. You can contact the bird owners, visit them and bring back the bird that you think is perfect for your home.

There are also several rescue shelters where the birds have been removed from abusive homes. These birds are given all the care that is required to bring them back to the best of their health. They are also treated for ailments if any. If you adopt from these rescue homes, you may get the bird for free. In some cases, you will have to pay for the care that has been provided to the bird after its rescue.

One or more?

This is a common dilemma for most of the first time buyers. Experts suggest that you bring home more than one bird, as Zebra Finches are highly social, requiring the company of other birds. It is best that you bring home a male and a female bird if you are bringing a pair home.

With birds of the same gender, the breeding season could be quite a nightmare considering that they will get very territorial. As we said before, you need to bring home an unrelated pair for maximum chances of a healthy breeding season.

For anyone who is buying Finches for the first time, the thumb rule is that the lesser the mutation, the cheaper the bird. You also have fewer chances of genetic disorders or issues with birds that have been bred normally.

From the time you make your purchase you are responsible for everything that the birds need to stay healthy and happy. Right from the drive to your home, you need to make sure that you take all the measures to keep the birds feeling safe and secure.

2. The bird's first day in your home

When you bring a Zebra Finch home, you need to realize that your life changes forever. You now have a big responsibility on your hands. You have to care for the bird, make sure that it is fed on time and is also happy in your home.

All of this can begin smoothly if you are able to get the first day of the bird in your home right. This day is very scary for the bird as he is moving into a completely alien territory. Until then, it is possible that your bird considered the pet store or the breeder's as his only world.

On the first day in your home, the bird is terrified. In addition to that, witnessing new faces of all your family members and friends will make it a little uncomfortable for the bird. In fact, you are also a new person that the bird is trying to comprehend. You will have to put in a lot of effort to make sure that you raise happy and confident birds.

If you are rehoming the bird, it is even more nerve racking as the bird has had his share of negative experiences as far as human beings are concerned. You will have to work doubly hard to make your bird regain his trust in human beings altogether.

You need to be extremely patient and consistent. In addition to that you will have to constantly gather information about your bird and specific bonding issues.

When you are trying to get your bird to become familiar with his new environment, there are two things that are extremely important for you to take care of.

a. The way home
When you bring your bird home, you need to keep the journey from the pet store or the breeders' to your home pleasant. Although pleasant is really not something that you can achieve, you can at least try to ensure that you keep your bird comfortable. Here are a few steps that you need to take:

- Place your birds in a carrier. If you are using a small box for the transfer, make sure that you have enough air holes for the bird to breathe comfortably.

- Drape a towel over the box of the cage to make the bird feel additionally secure due to the effect of darkness.

- You will have to make the floor of the cage or box non-slippery. This will ensure that the bird does not slip around the box as you drive. You may simply place a towel to make this happen for your bird.

- Secure the carrier. If possible, put it in some place where it will not move around. The passenger seat is the best option as you can also secure it with a seat belt.

During the drive home, you need to ensure that the box or cage is never placed in a crammed space such as the boot of the car or the dashboard. The latter will kill the bird thanks to all the exhaust fumes.

b. The cage
When your bird is home, you need to make sure that he has a temporary shelter that has been set up to keep him feeling safe and secure.

Where you place the cage makes all the difference. In case of smaller birds like Finches, the travel cage and the permanent enclosure can be the same, unless there is an aviary that you want to release the birds into.

If you need to transfer your bird from one cage to the other, just keep the door of the travel cage facing the door of the actual enclosure and wait for your bird to take the step into his new home.

Here are a few things that you need to keep in mind when you are setting up the cage of the new bird:

- Make sure that it is in a place that is quiet but still adjacent to all the activities of the family. The bird should be able to see you and your family but should not be in the middle of any commotion.

- The cage should be rested against something to make the bird feel comfortable. The best option is to keep the cage against a wall. That way the bird will never be caught off guard and will not have to worry about someone creeping up on him.

- The bird shouldn't be in for any surprises. That means, any large furniture that may block your bird's view of your home should be accounted for.

- The bird should get enough sunlight but not direct sunlight. Make sure that the cage is not directly in front of a window. This may overheat the bird.

- If the cage is near the window, however, it is a great way for your bird to stay entertained.

- The kitchen is the worst place for a bird cage. The bird may be exposed to several fumes as well as smoke that can be fatal. The fumes from non-stick cookware, especially can be very dangerous.

- You do not have to worry about getting your bird many toys on the first day. In fact, if you are bringing the bird home from the breeder, you may want to take an old toy back to help your bird have some sort of familiarity in the new home.

- Line the cage with enough substrate. On the first day, it is likely that your bird may poop several times making the cage dirty. This is primarily because of the anxiety of being in a new place.

Once you have taken care of all these steps, the rest is up to how you interact with the bird and how the bird perceives you and your family. The time that the bird takes to get accustomed to the new home depends upon each individual bird and the history of the bird's relationship with human beings.

3. Helping the bird settle in

Even though Finches are small birds, you need to ensure that their cage is not too crammed and small. To make your Zebra Finch feel completely at home, you need to keep some food available to the bird as soon as it is in your home. You can provide the bird with the same food as the breeders and the pet store. Even if your bird is primarily on a seed diet, you should not make any changes on the first day. Also keep a dish of water ready, although Finches are known for going on for days without any water.

If you already have a few birds at home, make sure that your new bird is kept away from them for health reasons. Quarantining is a must. We will learn in depth about this in the following section.

Finches are naturally very timid birds and tend to be quite shy as well. If you give them too much stimulus, it may really scare them and turn out to be hazardous. Let the birds take their time to settle in. If your bird seems too quiet and nervous, let him be.

Finches will only become active when they are comfortable with their new environment. Until then, you need to make sure that the area that they are in is calm and quiet. The interactions at this point should happen at face level. Never tower over the bird as they will begin to view you as a predator and will take a lot more time to trust you.

Choosing an outdoor aviary for Finches is not the best idea in the beginning. They will be too overwhelmed. Make sure that you house your birds inside your home. The way you house your bird also plays a big role in how your bird will respond to you.

The thumb rule is that you need to keep your distance from your bird for at least 72 hours after he arrives. While this does not mean that you should avoid the bird completely, it does mean that it is not yet time to show your bird off.

Make sure that no strangers interact with the bird during that time, loud music, partying and too much commotion should be avoided entirely.

When you do interact with your new bird, make sure that you are extremely gentle. You can only whisper to your bird and treat the bird like you really respect him.

There are several things you can do at this time to keep your bird engaged. Reading the newspaper, singing out songs softly and just talking to him about your day can be of great help. Make sure you maintain eye contact with your bird throughout. This helps them gain more trust with you and will ease the process of settling in.

Physical contact at this point should be avoided completely, even if your birds have been hand reared. Make sure that you only change the food, liner and the water in the cage. This should also be done very calmly and slowly. Every move should be deliberate and minimal in interaction.

The bird may move away from you, may show signs of aggression or may seem to actually run for cover when he sees you. This does not mean that your bird dislikes you. It is only an indication that he is trying to gauge and understand you.

With each day, you will see that your bird gets more and more comfortable around you. You need to stay persistent in your interactions in order to win him over.

4. Finches and other pets

If the Finches are your first pet, then all you really need to focus on is your new birds. However, if you are a parent to other pets as well, you have to make sure that you take care of the safety of your new birds as well as your existing pets.

Never take the personality of your pet for granted. Even the gentlest cat or dog can be very aggressive with pet birds. If you have birds as pets, too, you need to check if they are compatible with one another or not, before you put them together.

You have to understand that these are animals with instincts. They all have a role to play in the ecosystem and will live up to it even if they are domesticated. If one animal is a prey animal and the other is a predator, the latter will always overpower the former. They will have that instinctive sense towards their prey and may attack when you least expect them to.

a. Finches, dogs and cats

Finches are really tiny birds, which makes them a lot more vulnerable than a larger bird such as a cockatoo. When you are bringing a Zebra Finch home to a house with pets like cats and dogs, you need to follow these safety guidelines to make sure that there are no accidents.

- Make sure that they are aware of each other's presence. Do not keep the birds away from the cats or the dogs all the time. When your bird is slightly accustomed to the new home, you can take the cage into the same room as the family cat or dog.

- If you have a cat or dog at home, the cage should be heavy and strong enough. Make sure that your cat or dog is not able to knock the cage over and get to the bird.
- When the cage is big, the bird is able to back up in case your pet is able to get his paws through.
- The cage should have several visual barriers in it. This includes roosting areas, large toys or even branches. That way the bird is able to hide in case he feels threatened. Even if your bird is not breeding, providing a nest box might be a good idea for his or her safety.

Even after taking all the possible precautions, you need to make sure that your bird and your pet are not left entirely unattended. There should be no interactions that are unsupervised, especially if your dog or cat isn't trained.

If you intend to leave your cat or dog alone with the pet, make proper introductions. When your pet stops showing signs of curiosity towards the cage of the bird, it means that he is accustomed to having him around.

This is when you can let the bird out in your presence and see what happens. You must have the dog or cat trained to "stay" or you must have the bird trained to "step up". Without this, you are only asking for a disaster.

Some owners are lucky that their pets and birds get along like two peas in a pod. Even if the bird does get out of the cage, it is not really a risk as the cat or dog may not even pay any attention. But, if you notice the slightest sign of aggression in your cat or dog towards the bird, do not attempt to leave them without any barriers.

This is when the cage becomes even more important. Now, even if your bird and pet are able to stay with one another without any physical stress, you need to stay on guard. This is because the size of birds, especially Zebra Finches is a lot smaller than your cat or dog.

While your pet may not intend to harm the bird, accidentally stepping or pouncing on the bird may be fatal. Bites of cats, especially, are toxic for birds. Needless to say, you can imagine the impact that a dog's bite would have on the body of the bird.

If you do have untoward accidents despite all the precautions, remember that it is not the fault of your pet. They act purely based on their instincts. While preparing your birds and pets for one another is a seemingly wonderful idea, it is certainly not fool proof.

Experts recommend that you keep your pets and birds separated with some barriers. You may keep your dog or cat in an enclosure or you may want to get a good quality cage for your bird. The latter is always the better option. If you have an aggressive breed at home, make sure that you put both of them in enclosures when you leave the house for maximum safety.

Can you train your cat or dog to like the bird?

This is something that you may wish for as an owner. Of course, it is adorable to watch cats, dogs and birds play with one another. You can train your pet to understand what behavior is acceptable around the bird and what is not. But you can definitely not train them to lose their natural instincts. That is always the factor of doubt as far as pets are concerned.

Here are a few things that you may do if you are trying to train your cat or dog:

- Introduce the birds when they are younger. That is when the bird is more comfortable. If the bird is older, you will need to be able to handle the bird confidently before you start training the cat or dog. Just hold the bird up to the dog or cat and watch the reaction. If either one is uncomfortable, put the bird back and try again after a few days.
- If you notice your cat or dog trying to scare the bird or is putting the bird at risk with any action, you need to put an end to it instantly. A loud "NO" or stop is good enough for your pet.
- You must never allow the cat or dog to climb over the cage or attempt to reach into it.

- It is easier to train your pet when they are younger. Kittens and puppies are usually not aggressive. But, their playfulness can be hazardous to your bird. If the pet pounces on your bird, it could lead to serious injuries and even death in extreme cases.

When you raise your cats and dogs together, they are usually not aggressive. However, even the slightest provocation could be dangerous. For instance, if your bird is hormonal or brooding, he may become a lot more territorial than you expect.

This aggressive behavior during the breeding season is seen in females, especially if they have not been paired. In such cases, the attack may be initiated by the bird. If your dog or cat responds as a defense mechanism, it could still be fatal to the bird.

It is up to you to make sure that you understand any signs of behavioral changes in either animal. Unless pet owners are watchful and mindful of what their birds or cats are up to, interactions could be unpleasant.

That said, you also need to make sure that you train the bird to understand what behavior is acceptable and what behavior is not. The most important thing to do with Finches is to ensure that they do not learn the habit of chewing. If they develop the urge to chew, they may even make the ear of the cat or dog their target and get into trouble. If you notice your bird reaching for the paw or the ear of your pet, put him back in the cage. This tells them that this behavior is not acceptable.

Whether you want to train your cat or dog to be around the birds or not is entirely a personal decision. Some owners never let their birds out of the cage in the presence of their other pets.

The only reason that training is recommended is to ensure that there are fewer chances of accidents if someone leaves the cage door open accidentally or if the bird flies out during the feeding or cleaning session. Training your pet makes them less interested in the bird over time and this is imperative in making accidents in the household less common.

b. Finches and other birds

Finches are timid birds, no doubt. However, not all varieties of Finches are compatible with one another. Some of them can get really aggressive when kept in a mixed aviary.

With respect to Finches, a mixed aviary refers to different types of Finches and not different species of birds entirely. The rule of thumb with Finches is that they are best when kept with birds that are of the same physical structure as them. This includes Canaries and other Finches. Large birds like Parrots or Cockatoos may not be the best option if you want to house the birds together.

Compatibility among Finches is best understood when you study the nature of the birds in the wild. If they are social birds that are not restricted to pairs, then they will most likely get along well. However, if these birds get too territorial during the breeding season, you may want to study a little more about them before you keep them together.

Zebra Finches are usually categorized as pushy birds. This means that they can be kept in large aviaries with other birds like Canaries as long as there is a good visual barrier between them. Zebra Finches have the tendency to harass other birds unduly, making it very risky to have them together without these barriers.

It is best that you house your birds in pairs if you are going to keep them in a mixed aviary. You must at least ensure that there are equal numbers of male and female birds. That way the competition during the mating season will reduce, leading to less aggression.

If you already have an aviary or even a pet bird at home, the first thing you need to do is quarantine the new bird. You see, birds tend to be carriers of several diseases that can affect the whole flock. Even a seemingly healthy bird may develop health problems after the incubation period of these disease-carrying microbes is completed.

The new bird must be kept in a separate cage in an entirely different room for at least 30 days. This is the incubation time of most of the parasites and microbes. If your bird shows any signs of illness within this period, you may return him to the pet store or the breeder if you have a valid health guarantee.

A health guarantee is normally provided for 90 days after the purchase of the bird. However, you need to make sure that the bird is checked by an avian vet within 72 hours of purchase.

The quarantining room should have a separate air source. This means, you can keep the new bird indoors if the other aviary is an outdoor one. It is best that you keep the new bird in a different room altogether. Some even recommend asking a friendly neighbor to keep your new bird for a few days.

Make sure you handle the birds that are already in your home before you handle the new bird. This includes feeding, changing water containers etc. If you do handle the new birds first, take a shower and change your clothes and shoes before you handle the existing birds.

During this time you may want to treat your new bird for parasites such as coccidian, giardia etc. Stoll samples not more than 42 hours old should do the trick.

After quarantining, you can bring the cage of the new bird into the same room as the other birds. If the other birds are larger birds, it is best that you do not house them in the same enclosure. If they are Finches or Sparrows, you will have to observe the birds well before you place them together.

Once you keep the cages in the same room, observe the reaction of the other birds. Do they become irritable and aggressive? If yes, you may consider keeping them in separate enclosures. However, if the other birds merely respond to the calls of the new bird, which will make them noisier than usual, it may not be such a bad idea to introduce your birds.

You can introduce the birds by putting them in a neutral enclosure. That way, neither bird is territorial and aggressive. Individual interactions starting with the least aggressive bird is the best option.

Once all the birds in your aviary have been introduced to one another, you can try to place your new Finches in the mixed aviary too. Even the slightest sign of aggression means that you need to get your new bird out and house him separately.

There are a few things that will help you decide if certain birds will be compatible or not. First, you need to understand the habitat of the bird. Birds that are comfortable feeding off the floor of the aviary will usually be less aggressive. On the other hand, if the bird species has special requirements with respect to the feeding area, the nesting spot, etc, they are aggressive.

These birds tend to hijack the nesting areas of other birds leading to a lot of confrontations and aggression among one another. If you do have such birds in your aviary which includes the java sparrow, diamond fire tail finch, cut throat finch, red brown finch or the crimson finch, it is best that you do not mix your birds.

When you house mixed birds in one cage, you are creating a colony. So, always ask your vet or breeder if a certain species is a colony bird or not. Zebra Finches, for example, are successful colony birds. But, if you mix them with other species that aren't, you will be putting your birds at risk.

Even with successfully colonized birds, making sure that they get their individual space is mandatory. This means that each bird should have at least 2 cubic meters to himself. They also need to have their own perches and toys and also feeding containers that are easy to access and use. That way, you will have a peaceful colony of birds.

5. Pros and Cons of Zebra Finches
Now that you have decided to bring a Zebra Finch home, you will be happy to know that there are some wonderful reasons for bringing the bird home.

At the same time, there are several thoughts and notions about these birds that makes them easy targets for abuse. In fact, many Finch owners may be subjecting their birds to abuse without even realizing it.

So, no matter what you do, make sure that you pay attention to your bird despite what you may hear or read about Finches. Most people believe that these birds do well without any interaction. The reason for this is that the reaction to lack of interaction is not as dramatic as birds like the Parrots when it comes to Finches.

They will seem to be okay with being in a cage all day with a regular supply of water and food. This is entirely false as these birds have a wonderful personality that you can only learn about when you begin to understand their needs.

For those who are seriously considering Finches as pets, here are a few pros and cons of having them in your home:

a. Pros

- Care for Zebra Finches is very straight forward. If you provide them with a good housing facility and the right diet, they will stay pretty much healthy. They only need seeds, greens and enough vitamins to survive.

- There is so much variety with these birds. As we have seen in previous chapters, colors and sizes vary giving you the option of a wide range of birds in your aviary.

- Breeding them is extremely easy. They are prolific breeders in captivity. In most states, you do not even need a license to breed these birds.

  As long as you ensure that these birds have the right diet and healthcare, you will have regular breeding seasons with offspring being produced very easily.

  The only decision you need to make is whether you want to breed them or not. If you believe that you can provide the offspring with a good home, either through purchases or adoption, breeding Zebra Finches is a great idea.

- These birds can be tamed very well, albeit not easily. Once you have formed a bond with your bird, be prepared for a lot of singing and physical interaction. These birds are extremely entertaining and make wonderful pets.

b. Cons

- Zebra Finches can be excessively aggressive during the breeding season. If they have the right conditions to breed, they will definitely become dominating and may even fight with one another despite living peacefully in an aviary for several months.

- There is a lot of potential for misguidance when it comes to Zebra Finch care. You may find several blogs and websites about these birds. However, unless you have some legitimate source for the information provided, do not take it as the final word. These birds are so commonly found that people may just be imparting "wisdom" from what they have heard. If this information is wrong you could harm your birds.

- These are hardy birds but they are prone to certain conditions like avian pox and air sac mites.

  The worst thing about these birds is that they tend to hide the symptoms. Even with vet visits, it is hard to diagnose them in some cases. They may develop infections by just leaving the house as well. These birds are susceptible to heart attacks and will even thrash themselves against the wall of their enclosure if they are scared.

- Pet shops have created a rather questionable trend in the buying and selling of these birds. Because of the high demand for these creatures, you may find them in almost every pet store. However, some of these stores maintain the birds under terrible conditions. Genetic information may not be available to you as well.

  If you are able to buy a Zebra Finch for $2 or so in any store, you need to worry about the health of the bird. Such birds are very poor in quality and will most often not make it past one week of being in your home.

- They will mess up the cage. These birds tend to poop frequently and specifically inside the cage. You will have to clean the cage more often with these birds than you would do with birds like Parrots or Macaws.

- Breeding is taken for granted. Since these birds breed easily, many owners get into the practice without understanding the gravity. This means that they will not be able to provide proper care and diet and will also be unable to find homes for the offspring. If you are thinking of breeding your Finches, research completely to understand what exactly you are getting into in the first place.

There is no doubt that Finches are great birds to have at home. But, you also need to understand the financial commitment that comes with the bird despite the low cost for the bird itself. You will still have to invest in housing, care, healthcare, diet etc. for your bird to thrive well. In fact, this is a mistake that most owners make leaving their birds on seed-only diets, making them unhealthy and even obese in some cases. Even a bird as inexpensive as a Finch is a big responsibility.

That said, Zebra Finches are among the best option for a first time pet. If you have kids at home, a Finch is a great way to teach them responsibility towards their pet. Since the bite of a Zebra Finch is not hard, it is also safe to have the bird around children without a second thought. These birds are also not as demanding as birds like Parrots, making them hassle free as well. Caring for this bird will become second nature over time, as it is that simple. However, you need to keep improving your knowledge about your bird in order to make sure that you give him the best care.

Chapter 3: Zebra Finch Care

Once you have decided to bring a Zebra Finch home, making sure that you give them complete affection and care is your responsibility. Although these birds are not as attention seeking as Parrots or Macaws, it is not possible to keep them happy with no interaction at all. Remember, these birds are social in the wild and will need some sort of company in order to thrive.

In this chapter we will discuss about the basic needs of these birds that will make sure that you are able to provide a happy home for them.

1. Understanding Zebra Finches

It is wrong to underestimate a Zebra Finch for not being as intellectually developed as Parrots. These birds may not be as analytical, but depict other intellectual skills that prove that they need as much mental stimulation as any other pet bird.

To begin with the personality of the Zebra Finch is extremely versatile. These birds make great pets but thrive better as aviary birds as they love the company of other birds. If you want to have a "pet" Finch, it is best that you opt for hand-raised birds. These birds have learnt to associate food with humans and are more likely to form close bonds with their human friends.

It is easier to train hand-fed birds to come to you when called, perch on your shoulder and have a good time in your presence. These birds love to be around you and will not want to be put back in their cage for several hours. In case of handfed Finches, you can expect better temperament than the parent fed ones.

Of course, this does not mean that parent fed Finches are a complete no-no. They have their own unique way of exhibiting their personality. These birds are better for aviaries and it is a wonderful pass time to watch these birds interact with one another.

You will be able to point out the distinct personality and behavior of each bird when you observe them, The pairs that have bonded with one another interact in a loving manner and are pure joy to watch. They are also quite playful and enjoy jumping from one perch to another. They will preen themselves, sing to you, bathe in the water bowls and depict antics like hanging from the perches.

As for the cognitive abilities, Finches are among the most developed birds in terms of the neurological function. In fact, these birds can dream just like human beings! The patterns of neural activity that occur during sleep are identical to the neural activity that occurs while singing.

That said, it is no surprise that singing is a very important activity for Zebra Finches. In fact, these birds are able to showcase a lot of versatility in their singing. It is also a sign of good health and a way for the birds to attract mates.

Zebra Finches are known for their amazing vocal abilities. In fact, they are able to modify their tone so well that it matches the audience that they are singing to. Male Finches have special cells in the brain that allow them to produce original songs. These cells regrow every breeding season.

This vocal ability of the birds develops through various stages. In case of Zebra Finch chicks, you will only hear random sounds or babbling. Then each bird slowly develops his own song. These songs help the flock identify individual birds!

These birds master skills such as singing in a falsetto, trilling and warbling that takes people years of practice. This skill, sadly, goes unnoticed by human beings in most cases. But, the female Zebra Finch does not ignore the efforts of the male birds.

She recognizes the effort and is willing to commit to a bird that is able to perform these wonderful vocal modulations for a lifetime!

So, it is quite clear that Finches are highly developed creatures in terms of their neural activity and cognitive abilities. But, the needs of these birds are very limited. All they need in order to thrive are good housing, good food and social interaction.

If you are successful in providing all of the above, you can call yourself a good Finch parent. There are a few basic rules and requirements that you need to keep in mind while making arrangements to bring home a Zebra Finch and keep him healthy for life.

2. Housing Zebra Finches

The first thing you need to ensure your Finch gets is lots of space to fly around and really spread their wings. This is because these birds cannot manage any other form of exercise such as climbing on cages. So, when you are setting up your bird's permanent home, you need to be very aware of the space you are providing.

The size of your enclosure must be at least 30 inches in length for a pair of Finches. You should worry about the length more than the height of the cage. The rule of thumb is that the length MUST be greater than the height.

The distance between the cage bars also matters. Since these birds are small in size, the spacing between the bars should be between ¼-½ inches. If the cage is wider or narrower than this, you put your bird at the risk of injury.

Make sure that the cage is made from material that is non-toxic and durable. You should also be able to disinfect this material easily. The ideal option is aluminum. It is best if you can get a cage made from aluminum with a PVC powder coating. You also have the option of plastic coated cages. These cages are easy to clean and will also come in a range of colors.

The next thing to keep in mind is the design of the enclosure. No matter how fancy the cages may be, if they are not accessible, you will not be able to maintain them well. Every nook and cranny of the cage should be easy for you to clean. The cage door should be positioned in a manner that allows you to reach out for the bird when required. You must also make sure that you may be able to add more birds in the future to avoid the ordeal of transferring your birds to new cages.

It is always a good idea to keep Finches in pairs, as they need the company of another bird in order to thrive. In case you decide to have more than two birds, you also need to remember that one of them will be dominant and may attack cage mates that are submissive. The best way to ensure that this is avoided is by accessorizing your cage well and making sure that the birds have ample visual barriers to keep themselves safe from any attack.

a. Number to size ratio

There are a few rules that you need to follow when choosing the size of the cage that you want to keep your bird in. There is a value called the bird number to size ration. In case of Finches, you should be able to provide about 3-4 inches of floor space for every pair of birds that you want to house.

The height of the cage is not really important, as it does not really interfere in the personal space of each bird. What is important to note is that the movement of Zebra Finches is mostly horizontal and rarely vertical.

Of course, if your cage is very tall, the birds will like to take the highest perch to rest themselves. This is the only vertical space that the birds will fight for. In general, Finches will opt for the perches and the vertical space if they do not have ample floor space to move around in.

The ideal size for a cage for your Finches is 6ft x 2ft x 3ft (length, depth and height). This should be able to accommodate three pairs of birds easily.

Here are some things you must NOT do when you are buying a cage for your Finches:

- Do not go for enclosures that are too decorative and intricate in design.

- Make sure that the cage does not have many crevices that will be difficult for you to clean in the future.

- Cylindrical cages should be avoided, particularly ones that are small in their diameter.

- There should not be any gaps that may trap the feet of the birds.

- Watch out for paint that may peel off from the cage or from the perches or other items on the cage.

- Do not get any decorative items that use treated wood as they may harm the bird.

You have the option of building your own flight cage in case you do not want to invest in large cages that can be very expensive.

b. Building the enclosure on your own
There are various types of aviaries that you can build including outdoor aviaries or full wire aviaries. The designs and plans are easily available on the Internet. However, you need to have some basic considerations before you actually construct an enclosure for your bird.

You can get a wire enclosure constructed for as little as $10 and this is the most economical option available. This can be a super fun project. All you will have to do is dedicate a little time towards it.

The best type of aviaries to build are the free standing ones and not the permanent ones. That way it is also easy if you decide to move. Now, the only thing you need to remember with any permanent structure is that you may have to get permissions from zoning departments in your area.

Here are a few things you must consider before you construct an enclosure for your birds:

- Make sure you find a good location that is free from any traffic and noise.

- You should have access to water and safe electrical outlets.

- If the enclosure is indoors, you need to make sure that you give the birds ample air flow in order to be healthy.

- Indoor enclosures should be built in a way that they are easy to clean.

- You need to make sure that an outdoor aviary has good drainage. This will ensure that there are no damp floors, which may lead to disease.

- In case of the outdoor aviaries, it is also important to ensure that the area is safe from any pests or predators.

- As discussed before, the enclosure should be longer and not taller. You need to be able to provide ample floor space to each bird. A simple measure of 4 sq.feet per pair should help you understand the size of the aviary.

- The cage door is the trickiest part of the enclosure. You need to make sure that it is easy to access while keeping the birds safe from any chance of escape.

After you have taken care of all these considerations, the next thing to do would be to make sure that you get the right material to construct the enclosure with. Here are a few tips to help you with that:

- You can get all the material that you require from any home development store.

- The material that you purchase should be safe and must be free from any toxins.

- It is best that you avoid the use of redwood, cedar and screen wood. Pressure treated wood should also be avoided.

- Any material that corrodes, such as brass or copper, should be avoided.

- Zinc and lead may lead to heavy metal poisoning. These elements are usually found in the paints used to construct the cage.

- If you must use galvanized hardware cloth, make sure that it is washed with vinegar fully.

- Furniture polish and metal polish must be avoided at all costs when you make the enclosure.

- It is a great idea to get PVC powder coated wiring because of the ease of maintenance.

- Plastic netting is only suitable for indoor cages, as the outdoor ones will have rodents chewing into them in no time.

- Wiring should not have spacing more than ½" and less than ¼".

- Never use screens as the nails of the bird will get caught in it leading to serious injuries.

The only other rule that you must keep in mind is to make the cage as large as you can afford. That way, your birds will have a lovely permanent home that they can live for the rest of their lives in.

c. How to position the enclosure

The most important thing with the enclosure is where you position it. You need to keep the safety and comfort of the bird in mind at all times. One thing with birds is that they tend to get really nervous if you tower over them all the time. The best way to position these cages is such that the perches are above your own eye level.

If you have placed the enclosure indoors, it is a good idea to have the enclosure near a window that can give the birds natural light. You also need to have a shaded area in the enclosure that the birds can rest in.

You need to make sure that the settings of the cage mimic natural light as closely as possible. If you need to provide artificial lighting, it is best that you provide full spectrum light. You need to set these lights to a timer that switches it on at dawn and switches it off at dusk, basically matching the sun rise and sun set. You will have to make seasonal adjustments to match the length of the day.

Lighting is the most important thing for your Finches as it plays an important role in the hormone cycle of the birds. This influences breeding.

You can opt for fixtures that emit UV lights, as UV light plays an important role in vitamin D production and also calcium absorption in birds. You have to make sure that the cage is dark at night. Opting for a dim light is also a good idea to prevent any episodes of night fright.

There is no need to cover your cage at night. It has been discouraged by a lot of bird lovers and owners as it can reduce the amount of fresh air that your bird gets. Also, this may upset your bird's sleeping cycle as they may not wake up with the rising sun.

You need to give your bird a living area that is suitable for him. You need to keep the following points in mind to ensure that your home is bird-proofed properly:

- Do not keep any cleaning agents near the cage as they may contain ammonia and clorox fumes.

- The birds should be kept free from any chlorine fumes.

- Products that give out mists or fumes like air fresheners should not be placed near the cage.

- You should not have a combustion exhaust around the cage.

- Disinfectants containing pine oil should not be placed near the cage.

- Iron boards, heat lamps and pots containing Teflon should be kept away from the cage. When these surfaces are heated, they release a gas that is harmful for birds.

- Do not spray suede or leather protectant near the cage.

- Smoking near the cage area must be strictly prohibited.

- Be careful and watchful about gas link leaks.

- Moth balls should never be placed near the cage.

- Scented candles may contain fumes that are poisonous for birds.

- Varnish and paint removers should be kept away from the bird.

- You also need to make sure that the cage door is closed well whenever you leave the room.

- If you plan to let the birds out of the cage for long periods, it is essential that you do not have any fans or table fans around the area.

The area that you choose to house your birds in should not have temperature fluctuations. The kitchen is one such example. You should also make sure that the area is not accessible to your other pets and is also free from any toxic plants. You can get the birds acclimatized to any temperature that is comfortable for you. All you need to make sure is that it does not fluctuate too much.

If your birds are going to stay outdoors, shade is absolutely necessary. If you live in an area where the temperature fluctuates, the cage should be placed in an area that is protected from this fluctuation. The plants that are around your aviary should be non-toxic and bird friendly.

It is absolutely mandatory to keep free ranging birds away as they may contaminate the food of your birds and also spread infectious diseases.

With these tips and ideas, you should be able to find the ideal space for your aviary. That way your birds are not only safe but are guaranteed to be happy in the area that they are going to spend the rest of their lives in.

d. Accessorizing the cage
Stimulating the bird and making sure that he gets ample exercise is one of your biggest responsibilities. The perches and accessories of the cage are essential not only for the physical exercise but are also important for feeding the birds and giving them ample visual barriers of you have multiple birds in your aviary.

The type of perch that you choose plays a very important role. If you opt for dowel perches, you may face issues like lack of foot exercise as the bird may not get proper footing. These perches force the birds to shift all their weight on to one foot. As a result, in case there is an outbreak of bumblefoot, it may get aggravated.

Dowel perches may be included but should not be the only perch in your cage. Opt for perches that are made from nontoxic hardwood and clean material.

If you are planning to get a branch for your cage, make sure that it is obtained from a tree that has not been sprayed with any pesticides. Wood rot and mold should also be considered when you are bringing wood from the outdoors. The best option is to purchase manzanita branches that you will find in any pet store.

Although some people may tell you that sandpaper covered perches are good for your bird as it keeps the toe nail short, you must never opt for this. It leads to foot infections and bruises.

You must also place the perches such that they are not directly above one another or directly above the food and water bowls. This prevents any chances of contamination due to the droppings. Make sure that perches made of wood are replaced regularly as they become contaminated with time.

The next most important cage accessories are the food and water dishes. The only thing you need to remember is that these dishes should be very easy to clean. The best option for Zebra Finches is a stainless steel cup. Metal containers having soldered ends should be strictly avoided as they may lead to lead poisoning.

The water and food bowls should be placed away from one another to encourage exercise. If you notice that your bird is nesting in the cups instead of feeding from them, you will have to shift to a tube style feeder.

You will not need too many toys for your Zebra Finches. These birds are not so demanding in this department as compared to Parrots. Adding a swing is a good idea as long as it does not get in the way of the bird's movements. It must also never strike the wall of the cage.

You may add other modes of entertainment in the cage including short strings tied to the roof of the cage. This string should not be made of small fibres and should not be too long as it may entangle the bird. About 2 inches is a good length for the strings.

Finches will also appreciate a place to roost in at night. A nest or a perch should do the trick. You can place it near the upper corners of the cage. If you make a roosting area with wood, avoid cedar and redwood or any other pressure treated wood. You can use shredded paper, coconut fibre or tissue paper. Remember that this roosting area will also encourage breeding among your bird.

The nesting or roosting area is not mandatory. However, if you have several birds in your aviary, getting sleeping tents for birds also gives them a good hiding area in case one or more of their cage mates become aggressive.

When it comes to accessories for Finches, less is more. You have to make sure that the area is not too crowded. Flight should be comfortable as this the most preferred form of exercise as far as Finches are concerned. This is also the most effective way of exercise for Finches.

e. Keeping the cage clean
The bedding that you choose is an important part of hygiene. You need to make sure that whatever you choose is highly absorbent in nature. Some of the best options for Finch cages include paper towels, computer paper, newspaper, paper bags, butchers' paper or just about anything that absorbs well.

Every night before you turn the lights out, you need to make sure that you take the substrate out and replace all the soiled layers.

The cages and perches should be cleaned out every week with mild liquid dish soap. You can scrub them well to make sure that any dry feces are removed entirely.

Disinfecting the cage once a month is essential. A weak solution of bleach that is about 1 gallon of water with ¾ cup of bleach should do the trick. This will get rid of all the organic substances including feces, food and feathers. You need to remove as much as you can manually before you apply this solution on to the cage.

Remove the birds from the cage when it is being cleaned. It is a good idea to have a small transfer cage that they can be housed in on a temporary basis. Bleach may be used only when the area is well ventilated. You should not use this solution on any metallic surface.

The cage should be dried fully before your birds are allowed into the cage. The birds must not come in contact with bleaching powder at any cost. You need to rinse the cage well and dry it in the sun before the birds are replaced.

Physical cleaning of the cage on a regular basis is one of the best ways to prevent diseases amongst your flock. One risk factor for the owners of birds is the inhalation of fecal dust and spores while cleaning the cage. This may aggravate respiratory problems if any.

The best thing to do would be to install an electrostatic type filter for the air. If your bird area has a central air system, you can prevent the transfer of pathogens.

Of course, all the food and water dishes must be cleaned every day. If you see any food in the bowls, you need to discard it and make sure that your birds get fresh food every single day. That will keep them healthy and will prevent the chances of any fungal or bacterial growth inside the enclosure.

3. Feeding Zebra Finches

There is no doubt that the food you provide is paramount in deciding how healthy your birds are going to be. You need to make sure that the food that you give your Finches mimics their natural diet.

In addition to that, you also need to keep track of all the nutrients that your birds require at different stages of growth and development.

Zebra Finches have a very high rate of metabolism. This is true with almost any bird that is as tiny as the Zebra Finch. In a day, a Finch will eat as much as 30% of their own body weight.

In the wild, the diet of Finches is very varied and is not restricted to only seeds. They are omnivores that also feed on smaller insects. The plant and animal matter that the birds consume plays a very important role in providing the nutrients required by the body of the bird. Just like human beings, the essential nutrients for birds include carbohydrates, proteins, fats, minerals and vitamins.

If you think that it is as easy as filling up a dish with bird seed and giving it to your bird every day, then you are highly mistaken. You need to learn all about the nutritional requirements of your Finches.

You have to substitute a seed based diet with one hat is balanced and appropriate for your Finches. Simple things like including an egg in your bird's diet on a regular basis can help.

Some owners may want to replace the seed diet with a pellet diet. This is a good idea as long as you pick pellets that are specially made for Finches. Colored pellets should be avoided as they contain artificial colors. Anything that is not natural should be avoided.

One of the best options for your birds is to give them organic pellets that are named "high potency mash". This is especially good for Finches. There are various brands that make great bird food. You can consult your vet for one that suits your birds the best.

You may find pellets slightly more expensive in comparison to seeds. That is worth the extra price as pellets provide a more balanced diet option. It is best that 70% of your bird's diet is made from formulated pellets. The rest should be only fresh foods.

You will be able to find several products that are made especially for Finches. If the packet says "recommended for Finches" do not pick it up blindly. You have to consult your vet.

In the case of Finches, there is no need to give them any grit. In fact, grit leads to health issues and complications. If grit is over-consumed, it can be fatal as well.

You may need calcium supplements for your birds. Cuttlebones are recommended as they are considered a rich source of minerals as well. However, it is good to avoid it, as there could be some cheaper makes that are actually toxic and full of chemicals. Some bird owners offer charcoal to their birds. This is a terrible practice as it leads to vitamin B deficiency.

When you buy pellets for your birds, be sure to check the expiry date. Stale products will harm the bird adversely. Even when you buy a new packet of pellets, it is best that you place it in the freezer to keep it fresher for longer. This reduces the chances of moth larvae or beetle larva developing in the food that is meant for your bird.

Every bird needs treats. These treats are essential when you want to train your bird to step up or to obey certain commands. The best treats for Finches include egg mix and spray millet. You must provide spray millet minimally. Finches may develop the habit of eating only millet when it is given too often. This treat has no nutritional value and may affect the health of your bird.

If you give your bird any moist food including egg mix, veggies and fruits, you need to make sure that it does not sit in the cage for more than two hours. These foods are contaminated very easily and the microorganisms contaminating them will also harm the bird. Make sure you remove any uneaten moist food as early as possible.

Your bird also needs a good source of drinkable water. Clean water should be given to them at all times in order to help them digest the foods and absorb all the nutrients.

If you are filling the water dishes with water collected from taps made from copper or plastic, allow the water to run for a while before you actually fill the container. That way any possible toxins in the pipe will be removed before you give the water to your birds. In some cities, the water contains disinfectants as well as algae inhibitors. If your city uses chemicals to cleanse the drinking water that is supplied, you may want to opt for distilled water for your birds.

You must never add any medication, disinfectant or vitamin supplements to the water that your bird drinks. If you add anything that is unnecessary, the flora of microbes residing in the tummy of your bird can also be washed off, harming the gastrointestinal tract.

Sometimes, medication also tends to settle out of the solution proving to be toxic for the bird. When vitamins are added to the water for long hours they get oxidized and are rendered useless. This also increases the proliferation of bacteria tenfold.

It is best to provide plain and distilled water to your birds. You must also make sure that any contamination should be avoided. If you notice any feces in the water, you must replace it immediately to avoid it being fouled by bacterial growth.

It is not enough to just change the water upon contamination. You must rinse the bowl, clean it and only then refill the bowl. This should be a daily practice in any case. However, when you find any dirt in the water you will have to do it as many times as necessary.

There is always a small film of bacteria that forms on the food and water bowls. If you are not regular in cleaning out the water and food bowls, it will lead to chances of several diseases amongst your flock.

You will learn in the following chapters that two key factors in keeping your birds healthy are hygiene and good nutrition. If you are able to keep these two aspects as your priority, you will certainly have a happy lot of Finches.

a. Food options

In this section we will discuss the several options that you have with respect to feeding your Finches. The pros and cons of each type of food will be discussed in detail to help you make the best choice for your birds.

Bird seeds

You have a host of different types of bird seeds that you can get. The best type of seeds to buy, if you choose to feed your bird seeds, is the premixed variety. If you are experienced with birds you can, of course, make your own mix. That way you can customize it as per the requirement of your birds.

In case you opt for a premixed seed bag, it is a good idea to pick up the special Finch bags. That ensures that the seeds aren't too large for your bird.

Seeds should always be fresh. You should make sure that there are no droppings of rodents or cobwebs in your seed bag. Bugs and larvae are the main issue when it comes to bird seeds.

The best way to judge is to smell the bag of seeds. In case it smells rancid, discard it right away. You can also apply a simple towel test to the seeds. You can fold a spoonful of seeds in paper and moisten it a little. In case of fresh seeds, they will sprout. If the seeds are stale or dead, you will not see any signs of sprouts.

Millet spray is a type of seed that your Finches will simply adore. The seeds are still present on the stalk and it is a great pass time for the birds to pull these seeds out and eat them up.

It is best that you reserve seeds for treats, especially millet spray. They do not have as much nutritional value as the other foods available for birds.

Pellets

Pellets are available in all pet stores and are a mixture of various ingredients. In theory, it is believed that pellets are able to provide all round nutrition for the bird and are enough as the only meal you give your birds. Of course, you need to supplement the food with a lot of fresh foods.

Like any other commercially available pet food, you will find various brands of pellets. If you are unsure of which one is best for your bird, you can consult an avian vet.

Whenever in doubt, all you need to do is read up about the ingredients mentioned on the packaging. Choose the brand that has minimum preservatives. You must also compare the nutrition content per serving.

Fruits and vegetables

Fresh food is a must for birds to thrive. Fruits and vegetables make up a large portion of Finch food in the wild. Therefore, it is essential that you include it in your regular diet as well.

Remember, fruits and vegetables provide the best source of minerals and vitamins for the birds. These foods are also lower in fats, making them the most suited option for your pet.

In addition to all of this, birds tend to adore the idea of eating fruits and vegetables because of the color of these foods. Each bird will pick his favorite fruit or vegetable. You will be able to understand this by offering all options and seeing which one excites your bird the most.

Make sure you provide your bird with organic produce. That way, you can be sure of minimal pesticide usage. You must also wash the fruits and vegetables thoroughly before giving it to your bird. Some bird owners suggest that you warm the fruits and vegetables slightly in order to make it easy for your bird to digest them.

You can provide almost all fruits and vegetables to your bird. However you must avoid avocado at all times, as it is toxic. It is also a good idea to avoid iceberg lettuce. Although it does not really cause any harm, it is of no nutritional value to your bird.

The best choice of fruits and vegetables include:

- Bell peppers
- Beets
- Apples
- Broccoli
- Butternut squash
- Cilantro
- Collard greens
- Carrots
- Dandelion greens
- Corn on the cob
- Mangoes
- Mustard greens
- Pumpkin
- Papaya
- Peaches
- Sweet potatoes
- Spinach
- Zucchini
- Tomatoes

Whenever possible give your bird fresh foods. Frozen vegetables may be given occasionally. However, these fruits and veggies do not provide as much nutrition as the fresh produce.

All fruits and vegetables that are large in size must be chopped well or grated before giving the bird any. As for leafy greens, leave them whole as your bird will love to pluck out pieces using his beak. This is a wonderful stimulation activity for your bird

Live foods

As discussed before, Finches are omnivores and it is a good idea to include some live foods in their meal if you are comfortable with the idea.

In case of some species of Finches like the Waxbills, live food is a must as it is required for breeding. In case of Zebra Finches, live foods can be treated as a supplement that the birds will really enjoy.

When it comes to live foods, the best options available to Finch owners are wax worms and meal worms. You can get these at any pet store. You can also give your bird crickets or silkworms. But, you will have to work towards obtaining these foods for your birds.

Mealworms are larval beetles that usually thrive in grains. These worms are great for older Finches but can be difficult to digest in the case of babies and juveniles.

You can obtain a small can of refrigerated worms from any pet store. These worms must be placed in a bag containing wheat bran or oatmeal. That way, you will be able to keep the mealworms alive with some source of food.

One important thing is to place a small slice of sweet potato on the top for some source of moisture. You can feed these worms to your birds in a bowl. Make sure that the worms are not able to escape from the feeding bowl. That way you can prevent the younger birds from eating them.

Wax worms are basically moth larvae. These birds resemble caterpillars and are soft and fatty in nature. This makes the wax worms easier to digest for your Finches. These worms cannot be stored unlike the meal worms.

Wax worms have a specialized diet which makes it hard for you to give them a source of food and store them. You must make sure that you feed these worms to your bird immediately after you have purchased them to prevent any stale foods.

With this you should be able to get a fair idea about the kinds of foods that you must include in the diet of your bird. You can mix up the food groups to make a fun meal plan for your bird. If you are unsure of what to give your bird or where to begin, it is best that you consult your vet. There are also several Finch groups and clubs that will be able to help you with the same.

The more variety of foods you provide, the more likely the Finches are to eat well. If your bird gets bored of the same old food, he may even refuse to eat any.

You can give your birds a few seeds, chopped vegetables, leafy greens, egg shells that have been boiled and cleaned and also supplements as recommended by your vet.

In case you decide to give your birds pellets, you need to make sure that it is a part of the daily diet. Fresh produce, as we have discussed should be removed from the cage if left idle. Your bird should never wallow in any filth. They should have access to clean food and drinking water at all times.

When you are giving your Finches any seeds, make sure you double check the bowls. These birds have a peculiar habit of eating the top most layer of the seed and leaving the hull behind. To an inexperienced owner this looks like the seed itself. So, they do not refill the food bowl at all. As a result, the birds will succumb to starvation.

Any abnormality in the feeding pattern should be observed. If you do not see your bird eating as before or if you see that he is overfeeding, you need to consult your vet.

Availability of food is a key factor in the breeding season. If food is not available, most of the mating rituals are incomplete. In addition to that, birds may not mate for the fear of starving babies after the eggs have hatched. When they have a constant supply of food, they are confident enough to mate and produce offspring.

One important thing to note is that you must never blindly provide your bird with supplements. Just as a deficiency can cause serious issues, excessive consumption can also lead to several complications in the health of your bird.

4. Basic Finch training

Even with birds like Zebra Finches, some basic training is required to make them easier to interact with. These birds are trainable to some extent and will respond to training if it is consistent and regular.

When you begin training a Zebra Finch, it is important to remember that they are not as human oriented as Parrots. So, it may take much longer to train a Zebra Finch.

Hand raised birds are certainly easier to train. However, all birds can be trained if you get it right in the initial period. When you start training is the most crucial thing. It is best that you start when your bird is fully settled in the new cage.

It takes about a week for your Finches to get used to their new home. These birds are categorized as "high strung" when it comes to training. So, you have to give them a lot of time to settle down.

Begin by getting the bird used to your hand. You need to place your hand in the bird's territory for some time. Offer treats like fruits or seeds when you do so. That way your bird will begin to associate your hand with positive reinforcement.

Repeat this till your bird is comfortable around your hand. There are chances that the bird will voluntarily alight on your finger if you try this consistently.

Finger training Finches

It takes a lot of time to finger train Finches. But considering that these birds live up to 15 years of age or more, it is an important skill to teach your bird to make sure that you are able to get them away from situations that could be dangerous for them.

Try the above mentioned process till the bird recognizes your hands as the source of the treat. The next step is to make sure that the bird comes to your hand and is willing to sit on your finger.

One trick that really helps is holding the treat just behind your finger and waiting for the bird to approach you. When the bird is comfortable enough, he will simply step up on your finger.

Continue this on a daily basis till your bird is sitting on your finger as soon as he sees it. The first step is to finger train your bird inside the cage before you actually let him out.

Getting the bird out of the cage
You need to study the body language of the bird. If he looks comfortable on your finger, you can take him out of the cage for a few minutes.

When you do this, you have to make sure that the area is safe for him. That means the doors and windows need to be shut, the fans need to be turned off and the pets in your household should be away from the area.

Take the finch out and keep him on your finger for a few minutes outside the cage. In case he decides to fly away, it is a good idea to keep the cage door open and stay close to prevent the other birds from flying out.

After a few minutes, the bird will want to return to his companions. Having a bird who is hand trained is easier to catch if he does not return on his own. That is why it is mandatory to carry out initial training inside the cage before you actually let him out. When he is back in the cage, give him a few treats to know that it is a positive space for him to go back to.

Show training
Showing Zebra Finches is a very popular hobby amongst the owners. These birds are extremely good looking and can bring you several laurels if you manage to train them for shows and exhibitions.

It is best to train these birds in pairs. They need to first learn about the show cage. It is best that you remove them from their regular enclosure then set them into the show cage without any distractions such as toys or accessories.

Then, watch the birds. If they are comfortable with one another, you can start training them to step up on your finger or on a perch. There are several other tricks you can teach your bird if you are really patient with them. They will learn to hop over obstacles with the simple target training method.

According to the Zebra Finch society, you need to watch out for feather plucking. If that occurs with your birds, it means that they are not compatible and need to be put into separate cages. You can try combinations of different birds to ensure that pairing is suitable and compatible.

Chapter 4: Breeding Zebra Finches

It is a joy to watch Zebra Finches breed and take care of their young. During the mating season, the male birds will sing to the females and begin the courting period. This is when he will also choose a suitable mate and perform the mating dance. When this ritual begins, it means that the birds are ready to breed. The male will attempt to mount the female after this dance and if she is willing, they will mate.

Zebra Finches are prolific breeders in captivity. They will breed quite readily at that. It is necessary that you provide the right conditions for the birds once they are mature and ready to breed.

Usually Zebra Finches mature really fast. They are ready to mate by the time they are 12 weeks old. However, many breeders recommend breeding them after 6 or 9 months in order to produce healthy offspring.

a. Creating the ideal breeding conditions

- Make sure that the breeding cage or the nesting area is in a quiet area. It should be away from any noise of traffic or people. This placement of the cage should not be changed till the breeding phase is complete.

- Even the breeding cage must be large enough to make the birds feel relaxed. It should give them ample place to move around and stay physically active. It is best to have a cage that at least measures 16x16x20.

- Plan for the fledglings as well. There will be about 10 of them in the cage if you have a successful clutch with all fertile eggs that hatch.

- It is advisable to have just one pair of birds per cage. You do not want them to become hormonal and territorial and actually cause any damage to one another in a breeding aviary.

- Zebra Finches require a nesting box that is fully enclosed. This means that the box must have just one opening for the birds to enter and exit. The best nesting box is made with a wicker basket. These are hard to clean however. You can bring a cardboard box as well in order to have an easy to maintain nesting box for your Finches.

- The nesting box should be placed high up in the cage so that the birds feel secure enough to lay their eggs there. If the bird does not like the nest provided by you, they will build their own with whatever material is available to them. If you see your birds building a nest despite giving them one that matches all the requirements, you need to just move it higher to see how they respond.

- The nesting material that you provide also plays an important role in the breeding season. This material should be completely clean. It must also be safe for the birds that are breeding. One of the best things to use is dried grass. This grass should be free from any fertilizer or treatment. You also get a type of cotton that can be used in the nest.

- Never keep any string near the cage. Birds are very curious and will want to play with the string. They may end up hurting or even strangling themselves in the process. If you do want to provide strings as a means of entertainment for your bird, make sure that they are short strings that do not measure more than 2 inches in size.

- You need to maintain a very good diet for birds that are breeding. They should be healthy enough to lay the eggs and hatch them. If they are going to raise the young on their own, they need as much nutrition as possible. Putting your bird on a seed diet is not enough. Mix up the food sources and include a lot of calcium sources such as crushed oyster shells, cuttlebones etc. Only when food is available in abundance will the birds breed. They need to feel secure enough to provide food to their young in order to breed.

- Light is another very important factor in breeding birds. Sunlight determines the production of various hormones in birds. In the case of Finches, they need about 14 hours of daylight in order to start breeding. If you are unable to provide a natural source of light to your birds, you can choose to give them a full spectrum light setup.

  Once you make all the conditions available to the birds, they will begin to breed. The male bird is responsible for making the nest. Even after you have set the nesting box up, you will see that he will add fibers, papers etc. to make the nest exactly the way they need it in order to breed successfully.

Once the eggs are fertilized, the bird will lay one egg each day. Usually, a clutch can contain between 3 to 10 eggs. Once all the eggs have been laid, the hen will begin to sit on it and try to hatch it.

In the case of Finches, the responsibility of incubating the eggs is shared by the male and the female. Although the female spends maximum time with the clutch, the male also helps in short intervals.

Ideally, the incubation period for Finches is about 14 days. It may extend to a maximum of 20 days. In case the eggs do not hatch even after 20 days, chances are that the eggs are not fertile. This is when you can take the eggs out of the nest.

The moment you do this, the parents will begin to prepare for their next clutch. In some cases, this process may begin even before the first clutch has hatched. If this happens too often, it is best that you separate the birds.

The separation serves a dual purpose. To begin with, the birds will get some time to regain their strength and replenish the nutrients inside their body. It is recommended that you do not allow the birds to lay more than 4 clutches in a row.

b. Artificially incubating the eggs
It is best that you allow the parents to hatch the eggs and then take over the responsibility of feeding the birds by hand in order to make them acquainted with people.

Artificial incubation is not always necessary. There are a few breeding problems that arise making it necessary for you to hatch the eggs in an incubator.

Egg breaking or eating
This is a common issue with birds that have been brought into captivity from the wild. This is only a result of the bird's defensive behavior towards anyone who approaches the nest.

The bird sits or jumps on the egg as an attempt to safeguard it and ends up breaking the eggs. This is when you have to take the following precautions:
- Increase the size of the cage or enclosure.
- Make the nesting box narrower and darker.
- Minimize any activity in the breeding area of the birds and make it as quiet as possible.

In some cases, this habit is repeated with every clutch and is actually just a learnt behavior pattern. This is when you will have to intervene and incubate the eggs artificially.

Abandonment of the eggs
Smaller birds like Zebra Finches are notorious for abandoning their eggs. You will face this problem more often with hand raised parent birds who do not have any parenting instinct. This is when you can take one of the following measures:
- Pair a hand raised bird with one raised by the natural parents. That way one is experienced and the other can learn.

- If your hen is not a good breeder, you need to take the decision of taking the bird out of the breeding program. While this may be hard for you to do, you need to understand that these birds are just not meant to care for a clutch.

- If your birds have been good parents in the past, then you need to check the nesting conditions that you have provided. If anything seems out of the ordinary or inappropriate, making necessary changes will prevent abandonment.

If you notice any of the above problems with the clutch, you will have to incubate the eggs artificially. Collect the eggs carefully and place them in a commercially available incubator. You will have the details of all the settings for Zebra Finch eggs. Once you have set the incubator as needed, you have to follow these measures to make sure that you get maximum hatchability with your eggs:

- Place the incubator in an area that is free from any direct sunlight or drafts.

- The incubator should be sterilized before you place the eggs inside. The web bulb wick and the humidifier must be functioning properly.

- Make sure you wash your hands and clean the eggs thoroughly before you put them in the incubator. They should be free from any dirt or grime.

- The small end or the pointed end of the egg should always be lower than the large end of the egg.

- The egg must be turned at least 5 times each day. If you fail to turn the eggs every day, chances are that the chicks that are developing will get stuck to one side and may be born with the organ sticking out of the body.

- Once you have set the eggs inside the incubator do not disturb them except for when you turn them. While doing so, if you notice that the eggs are still cold, chances are that you have not started the incubator or that it is not functioning properly.

- It is possible to check the progress of your eggs with a bucket of water. In the beginning the eggs will sink to the bottom while towards the end of the incubation period, they will begin to float on the surface.

Once the eggs have hatched, you need to shift the chicks to a brooder. You may choose to place the bird in a commercially available brooder or may make one using a box and the appropriate full spectrum light. The temperature should be around 92 degree F when the birds just hatch. By the 5th day you can reduce this to 80 degree F.

You will have to place absorbent bedding such as newspaper. Keeping the brooder moisture level above 50% is very important. If you are making a brooder at home, you can use a spray bottle to mist the brooder with lukewarm, distilled water. Make sure you only spray around the brooder and never directly at the chick.

c. Hand feeding your Finches

- You can get the feeding formula from any local pet store. Make a mixture of this formula with hot water and place it in a sterilized container. The formula should be made freshly before every feeding session and should never be stored in the refrigerator.

- Force-feeding chicks is strictly prohibited. If you hold up a teaspoon or a syringe to the bird, he should approach you voluntarily. This reduces chances of choking on the food.

- As the chick feeds he will bob his head up and down. You will have to match the rhythm of dispensing food with this rhythm.

- Pause and give the food in short intervals to help the bird swallow better.

- The formula must never fall on the nostrils of the bird. If you notice any on the beak or nostril, clean it immediately.

- Never overfeed the chick. If he stops eating do not force him.

- The crop should empty before you give the bird his feed.

Increase the consistency of the formula with each day. By day 5 you can start weaning the chicks. Leave the food around and see if they eat on their own. By the 8th day, you can stop feeding the bird at night. That will make them hungry enough to eat by themselves. By the time they are 21 days old, they should be fully weaned.

Hand feeding is a great option if you wish to sell the chicks. Most people prefer birds that are already used to human interaction in order to make it easier during the housebreaking phase. These birds are also much easier to train.

In some cases where the parents are caring for their young, you can try mixed feeding. Allow the parent birds to give the chicks one meal and you can give them the next until they are weaned. These are the most sought after types of birds as they have the experience of being parented and are also comfortable around human beings.

Chapter 5: Exhibiting Zebra Finches

While rearing Finches and breeding them make for a great hobby, several individuals also exhibit the birds in bird cage shows that are organized by Zebra Finch Clubs and Societies.

a. Preparing for the exhibition

The only challenge with Zebra Finches is exhibiting them in the most ideal condition. These birds are exhibited in pairs that share the same color. The birds have to be true pairs, which means that they should be compatible to breed with one another. This is what makes the task challenging.

Zebra Finches are not hard to pair per say. The challenge is the fact that these birds will molt or shed their feathers at any given time of the year. So even if you have the perfectly matched birds with the exact coloration, they may molt during the show season. In some cases the birds may molt after the show and in other cases they may retain the condition forever.

This has an advantage for exhibitors as well. If your bird has been fairing poorly for a week in a certain exhibition, in the following week, the birds that were in the lead may begin to molt giving your bird the perfect opportunity to get to the top.

Besides the coloration, the condition of the bird also matters when you are showing them. The size should match the standards that have been set by the society that is organizing a certain show.

It is up to you to bring out the best in your bird if you are interested in exhibiting them. It is best that the show birds are not housed in an aviary and are kept in their own individual enclosures. This reduces chances of feather plucking, injuries, feet defects due to constant stepping on the feces of other birds etc. If you allow your birds to get into fights, they may have deformities like missing toenails that will make them less likely to win a show bench. They may be awarded in individual categories, however.

Make sure you give your bird a good diet that will help him or her reach the show condition. Good quality food and nutritious diets will help your pair fare well. You can even bathe the birds with warm water sprays often to keep their feathers in good condition. You can also leave a bowl of warm water in the cage for the birds to bathe in. About 10 days prior to the show, you can use a heavy spray to clean up the birds.

Birds that are being exhibited must also be show trained. The only thing that Finches have to do is to be presentable on the show bench. They have to be trained to stay in a show cage for one hour. Some birds do not like to be exhibited and may end up with a feather plucking urge when forced to do so.

Even the cage that you are presenting the bird in should be of good condition. You should keep the cages clean and painted. Any repainting that is done 12 hours before the show leads to negative marking. You need to prepare the cage well in advance.

Exhibiting a bird is more than just winning medals and prizes. If you are able to meet more Zebra Finch owners, you will also learn about your own birds and may discover better options for keeping them healthy and happy in your home. Your birds will also be social and friendly when taken to these exhibitions on a regular basis.

b. Exhibition categories

If you are new to the world of Finch exhibitions, it can be confusing to figure out which category your bird fits perfectly into. There are different rules based on the coloration of the birds. Most of the mutations of Zebra Finches are recognized. However, you need to know which category your bird fits into in order to be successful in your exhibitions.

There are 12 categories according to the Zebra Finch Society in the UK. This is the standard that has been adopted in most countries that host regular Zebra Finch shows:

- Normal class: this is for birds that do not have any visual mutations. It includes the yellow beaked normal variety only.

- Fawn class: this category consists of birds such as the yellow beak fawns which do not display any other mutation such as isabel, penguin or pied visually.

- Pied class: this is a broader category that includes all specimens that show pied mutation on their plumes. However, the bird may not display other mutations such as grey cheeked, orange breasted etc.

- Silver class: this class consists of recessive and dominant silvers and also includes yellow beaked birds that do not display any other mutation.

- Cream class: this category includes recessive and dominant cream varieties that do not have any other mutation that is visually obvious.

- Lightback: this includes fawn and normal lightbacks including the recessive and dominant dilute forms of this mutation. They must not display any other mutation including orangebreast, blackcheek etc.

- Chestnut flanked white class: this class includes all varieties of flanked white birds and also yellow beaked varieties. Of course, the bird must not display any other mutation such as isabel and greycheek.

- White class: this includes all birds that are visually white. It also includes the pied varieties and the yellow beaked varieties. You cannot enter a crested variety in this category. You must also avoid birds that show any other form of mutation.

- Penguin class: this class includes all types of penguins including the yellow beaked birds. They include the dominant dilute penguins, the recessive dilute penguins, the normal penguins and the fawn penguins.

- Blackfaced and blackcheeked class: this class includes two of the most sought after mutations in Zebra Finches. It includes all blackfaced and blackcheeked varieties including pied, flanked white, cream, silver and fawn varieties. Crested, orangebreasted and blackbreast varieties are not included.

- Black and organgebreasted class: this includes all varieties of orange and blackbreast birds including the normal yellow beak varieties. It includes flanked whites, isabel, lightbacks, creams, silvers and pied that show this mutation.

- Crested, greycheeked, fawncheeked and isabel class: this includes all specimens that are crested and show the above mutations. However birds that also display orangebreast, blackbreast, blackface and blackcheek mutations are not accepted in this category.

In certain exhibitions, you will not see light, cream and silver as separate categories. A special class called the dilute class is created to combine these three mutations. You may also find fawncheeked, crested, orangebreasted, blackbreasted, blackfaced and blackcheeked categorized as "standard variety class."

c. Judging criteria
Judging is quite straightforward when it comes to Zebra Finches. These birds are judged by a panel of experienced breeders and Zebra Finch Society members. Some panel members may also have won these shows consecutively to become a part of the judging panel.

The judging itself is quite straightforward and the birds are usually judged based on two performances, one in the morning and one in the afternoon. Even if the bird performs extraordinarily in the morning, it is the afternoon that counts the most.

It is a little daunting when you enter a show that does not have several categories and actually includes several mutations into one class. This is when you need to be very careful with your presentation to grab the attention of the judges to the maximum.

Here are a few things that you can do to make the judging process more favorable to you and your bird:

- Make sure you get a good spot on the judging table. Having stewards to take care of each section is really useful to you.

- You need to make sure that your bird is exhibited in the right section based on category. Sometimes, the judges will overlook a pair of birds because they were placed in the wrong section.

- The birds that you present must be a true pair with the exact coloration. If you see any mismatch, do not enter the bird.

- If you are entering the bird as a breeder bird, then you should make sure that you get a breeder ring for your bird from the society organizing the contest. This ring is changed each year.

Once you have all this in place, the judges will be able to check for the finer points, which can actually earn the award for your bird.

The judging process in most cases is based on elimination. In fact, the birds are judged from the bottom upwards. The ones that have dirty cages or dirty birds are rejected first.

The next birds to go are the ones that have very obvious flaws in coloration based on the criteria that the bird has been entered in. If the birds have other features that are really good, they may be retained. This includes the type and the shape of the birds.

The eliminations continue till the last nine cages of birds remain. Zebra Finches are displayed in pairs and this makes it a lot harder for the judges. This is because a cage may contain a fantastic specimen of the hen and a poor cock or vice versa. If you have entered such a cage, your chances of qualifying depends entirely on the quality of the other birds on display.

After the final nine are shortlisted, the cages are placed side by side to compare the birds. The judging takes place with the categories in each mind. Once the judges have decided which birds fair on the top of the list, the entry is recorder to make sure that there are no last minute changes in the judgment passed by them.

In case your exhibit is disqualified for any technical reasons in the final round, the results may vary. After the first round of judging, the highest marked bird and breeder are retained. There is another round called the specials that usually takes place in the afternoon and is really important. You have to pay all your attention to this class.

The best bird is selected from each class. Now there are two types of entries- adult birds and breeder birds. In case the top position in one class is claimed by a breeder bird, then all the adults are specially judged to choose the best adult bird and vice versa. Now, this is the section where a lot can change for your bird. Even if they have been picked on top of the list to begin with, they may go lower after this round.

Many awards are given away in each show including Best Novice, Best junior, Best Champion, Best Zebra Finches etc. In some shows, the winners of one category may not be allowed to enter another category.

The judging is usually very methodical and you will be able to talk to your judges to understand how your bird fared and what improvements can be made in the future to help perform better. Judging is extremely detailed and you will be able to get a lot of inputs from them.

However, reserve your questions for after the show. Never speak to the judges during the exhibit. You must stay away from the judging table and allow the judges to present unbiased views on your birds.

d. Exhibiting your birds
There are several shows that you can enter your bird in. It is possible to locate at least one show in your city or close to your city through the websites of these organizations that hold the shows.

Here is a simple step-by-step process to enter your birds into any local or national show:

- To begin with obtain a schedule that is usually given to you by a show secretary. They can be contacted through the website of the organization.

- You will have to fill up an entry form to get your bird into the show. You can start by putting the bird in a "fancier" or "novice" class if this is your first contest. Make sure that you choose the class of the bird correctly from the options on the form. If you make an error, it cannot be corrected.

- In case you want to exhibit a breeder pair, you will have to get the appropriate breeder rings. Breeder pairs are those that you have bred on your own. The other category is the adult category.

- There is an entry fee that you will have to enclose with the entry form, this should be posted with a self-addressed envelope.

- After this is done, prepare the cage for exhibition. You need to obtain a cage that is approved by the rules of the show that you are entering.

When the final day arrives, make sure that you place the cages in a strong box to make it easier to transport. Clean water must always be available for your birds to drink. Of course, you also have to carry enough food as per the feeding schedule of your bird.

Chapter 6: Health Issues with Zebra Finches

The health of your bird is the most important aspect. Of course, you will take all the precautions needed as far as the health of your bird is concerned. However, the one thing that you need to be aware of as a bird owner is identifying whether or not your bird is in the best of his health or not.

This chapter talks about all the common symptoms of the health issues faced by Zebra Finches and the treatment methods for each of these health problems.

1. Identifying a sick bird

There are several symptoms that help you identify a sick bird. These symptoms can either be mild or intense. In any case, you have to be alert and identify the slightest change or deviation from normal. That can work wonders in saving your bird's life.

Here are a few symptoms that can help you identify illnesses in your birds and provide timely assistance:

- **Fluffed feathers**

  If your bird looks fluffy or puffed up in appearance, it is the most obvious sign of an ill bird. The common reason for fluffing up feathers is to keep himself warm.

  When your bird tries to do this, you will see that the regular sleek frame is lost. The bird will actually look fat and extremely messy. Sometimes, birds may just puff up their feathers for some time while preening. But if the puffiness is prolonged, it is a matter of great concern. However, puffiness must never be ignored even if the bird retracts the feathers when you approach him. This is a common defense mechanism, as the bird does not look vulnerable. You must also be observant of the bird's body language. If the bird looks sick or you have the slightest suspicion, you need to make sure that you pay attention.

- **Wet vent**

  If the vent area of the bird is constantly wet, then it can be considered a symptom of illness. This is the underside of the bird where the bird excretes from. If the bird is healthy, the vent is dry and clean.

- **Respiratory issues**
One of the most common tell tale signs of sickness in a bird is abnormal or heavy breathing. This type of breathing without any physical exertion means that the bird may be unwell. In addition to heavy breathing the bird will also exhibit tail bobbing.

If the bird is sneezing, coughing or has some sort of nasal discharge, it is an indication of illness. Hold the bird close to you if you have any suspicion. You may be able to hear a distinct clicking sound, which indicates chances of mites or parasites in the air sac. This needs to be checked immediately to help the bird recover at the earliest.

- **Inactivity**
Finches are usually quite active and love to fly about or just interact with one another. If your bird is sleepy all the time and is found catching untimely naps, it is a warning sign.

Birds will nap in the afternoons or during the day. However, they seldom nap when the rest of their cage mates are active. If your bird is snoozing while the others are active, you need to look at it as a warning sign.

Birds that sit at the bottom of the cage for long hours may also be unwell. This is not a common thing especially in an aviary, as Finches prefer to interact with one another and will seldom be isolated in this manner. If they have the habit of sitting on the floor of the cage, it will usually be with their partners.

However, if you see that your Finches are shunning the company of other birds, especially their own partners, you need to understand that there is definitely some problem with the bird.

- **Loss of appetite**
If a bird loses interest in food because of any illness, it is a sign of great concern. Always be observant of your birds. The thing

with Finches is that they do not want to appear unwell or sick. They may just pretend to eat the food you have given to them to make sure that they do not look vulnerable. However, they could only be sifting through the food and may not be actually consuming anything.

- **Lack of singing**
  Vocalization is the most important sign of health especially in Finches. These birds are known for their unique songs and vocalization patterns.

  When birds are unwell they remain unusually silent. The idea behind this is to make sure that they do not attract any unwanted attention from predators.

  In addition to this, birds that are unwell will also do this as a method of saving up on their energy. If a bird who normally loves to chirp and sing becomes abnormally silent, you must immediately take him to your vet.

- **Unusual droppings**
  Whenever you are cleaning out the substrate of the cage, make sure that you check the droppings of the birds. If the droppings are abnormal or have some unusual color, it could be a sign of indigestion or some disease.

  If you have several birds in your aviary that belong to different families and species, this can be a little challenging. However, you can watch out for a few basic things such as the urates, which should be white and dry in color. On the other hand if it dries up to look green or yellow, you need to show some concern immediately.

  Maintenance of Zebra Finches depends mostly on simple observation. In case you are unable to spend time watching your birds, you will never become familiar with the regular and normal behavior. As a result, you will also be unable to identify anything out of the ordinary.

In fact, you may miss out on initial symptoms of diseases that can be managed fairly easily. Even if you stop paying attention for a short time, you can miss out on some important behavioral changes that can be pivotal in saving the bird's life.

One thing all bird owners should know about is that birds prefer to hide their illness in order to look fit. In most cases, by the time the symptom becomes obvious, the bird is already very sick.

If you have an aviary, a sick bird is not only a matter of concern because of his health. He is a ticking time bomb that can affect the rest of the flock in no time.

If you are observant and find the symptoms early, you can have the bird quarantined and ensure that the rest of your flock is safe too. You have to first identify that your bird is sick. The next step is to narrow in on which disease it actually is. Lastly, you need to take all the preventive measures necessary for your aviary in order to keep the birds healthy.

2.Common illnesses in Finches

Like all species of birds, the Zebra Finch is also susceptible to attack and infection by certain microbes. These birds are genetically predisposed to certain conditions and you need to make sure that you take care accordingly.

There are other factors like nutrition and hygiene that also affect the health of your bird to a large extent.

a. Nutritional diseases

As discussed before, the metabolism in Finches is very high. As a result, their body also demands a lot of nutrients. Birds are quicker than any other creature in the animal kingdom to depict the signs of malnutrition.

In many cases, pet birds have been diagnosed with nutritional diseases more often. In most cases, the immunity of the bird towards disease causing organisms is compromised when his nutritional requirements are not met.

It is very common to see birds showcase nutritional problems when they are in the breeding cycle. Problems like calcium deficiency are most prevalent in these birds. This leads to a lot of complications like egg binding or prolapse of the oviduct.

Each species has a different type of response to deficits in nutrition. In the case of the Finches, you will see a lot of tell tale signs. The most common nutritional diseases in Finches include:

Obesity

This is the most common nutritional disorder, often ending in hepatic lipidosis or fatty liver. This condition has been observed in birds that are usually on a high fat seed-only diet. This type of diet also leads to other issues like lowered calcium in the blood. Seeds also lack nutrients like vitamin A.

Two organs of the bird's body that are normally affected by obesity are the liver and the heart. Over time, all the fat that has been accumulated in the blood is passed on into the liver. This leads to a drastic decrease in the amount of functional tissue in the liver.

This condition also makes the liver very enlarged. If the fat accumulation occurs around the heart of the bird, the normal functioning of the heart is also compromised.

If the bird is overweight, he is not able to perform simple tasks such as flying or bathing in the water trough.

Symptoms of hepatic lipidosis

- The fat deposits are seen on the abdomen and chest, making these areas look large and buxom.

- The beak tends to grow rather abnormally. This condition is often identified by those who groom the bird and trim the beak at the vet's office.

- You will see obvious black spots on the toenails and the beak. This is primarily because the functionality of the liver is compromised. The clotting of blood does not occur properly leading to bruise-like splotches on the beak and the nails.

76

- The liver is enlarged. Of course, this is not seen visually. When the bird is being checked by the vet, this becomes obvious. In smaller birds like Finches, you can see this enlarged liver through the screen if you just moisten the skin with some alcohol.

These clinical signs are noticed in birds of all species. If you do not curb the fat intake of your bird, the regular bodily functions are largely compromised. Even simple stress like a loud noise can be too stressful for the bird, leading to death.

Diagnosis

- Physical examinations are the first step to diagnosis.

- Your vet may also require the blood to be tested for anemia, lipemia or chances of jaundiced plasma, which indicate compromised functioning of the liver.

Treatment

The best way to manage this condition is by improving the nutrition of your bird. You can prevent this condition entirely if you are careful about what you are feeding the bird.

Make sure that your bird gets a good balance of homemade food as well as commercially available food for the best possible results.

Some medicines such as probenecid or colchicine can be administered to help birds who have been severely affected.

Hypovitaminosis A

This is yet another condition that you will see in birds that have been maintained on an all seed diet. Most seeds and nuts do not have any traces of vitamin A.

The mucous membrane and the epithelial tissue are maintained by Vitamin A. When the levels of this nutrient drop, resistance to pathogenic or disease causing organisms also decreases.

You will commonly notice infections of the sinus and the respiratory tract in birds that have a deficiency of Vitamin A. you will also notice scaliness, flakiness and thickening of the skin of the bird's feet.

Symptoms of Vitamin A deficiency

- White plaques are seen on the roof of the mouth.

- A change in the functionality of the tear glands and the salivary glands leads to high levels of oral mucous.

- Respiratory difficulty accompanied by problems like coughing are quite common in birds with this condition.

- When the lack of vitamin A leads to compromised immunity, it manifests in the form of abscesses in the respiratory tract, the crop and the oral cavity of the bird.

- In case of brightly colored birds such as Zebra Finches, the coloration of the plumage will also fade away with time.

- The hatchability rate of the clutches will decrease quite drastically.

- The chicks that do hatch may not survive or may fail to gain weight and die eventually.

Treatment

Preventive measures, such as a healthy diet and proper supplementation, are the best options for your bird. In case your bird develops this condition despite all the care, here are a few things that you can try:

- Provide commercial feed that is fortified with Vitamin A. These foods are often given along with water.

- The amount of orange and red vegetables as well as green leafy vegetables should be increased in your bird's diet.

- You can provide your bird with beta- carotene supplements. In most clinical cases this supplement is injected.

- Add a few drops of the extracts from a Vitamin A gel capsule into your bird's food.

- Cod liver oil can be added to your bird's diet. This is also quite easy to mix with dry foods like pellets and seeds.

With a balanced vitamin A intake, you will notice that your birds become more and more resistant to common health issues. You will also notice a very positive change in the reproductive cycle and results with regular Vitamin A supplements.

Hypervitaminosis A
Just as the deficiency of nutrients can lead to a lot of health problems, an excess of the same nutrient can be toxic to the bird. Many bird owners tend to over-supplement the diet of their birds leading to several complications.

The only sad thing is that this is a poorly documented condition among birds. In cases of other animals, it has been seen that an excess of vitamin A in the body leads to a lot of fatigue and weakness in the bird. It can also lead to pain in the bones.

Calcium, Vitamin D3 and Phosphorous imbalance
If the diet of your bird consists mainly of oily seeds and grains, you will notice these imbalances. These foods have a very low ratio of phosphorous to calcium and are also deficient in Vitamin D3. Additionally, the calcium that is available to the bird is bound within the body in the form of soaps when the diet is too oily.

Calcium is one of the most important minerals as far as the birds are concerned. The production of the egg is highly hampered when the calcium intake is not good enough. Calcium is also required by the skeleton of the bird. If calcium and phosphorous are not absorbed properly, it can lead to bones that are underdeveloped or extremely fragile.

There are several other body functions such as the transmission of nerve impulses, muscle contractions and also metabolic processes that are affected by the calcium levels in the body.

Calcium metabolism is affected by the amount of Vitamin D3 and phosphorous in the bird's body. Therefore, providing only calcium is meaningless, as it will not be utilized properly.

Ideally, the ratio of calcium to phosphorous should be 2:1 in the body of birds like Finches. This value can have a 0.5 variation and not more.

Symptoms of calcium, vitamin D3 and phosphorous imbalance

- Adult birds are highly uncoordinated in muscle function when there is an imbalance.
- Weakness is commonly seen in birds with this nutritional deficiency.
- Egg binding as well as paresis or fatigue is seen in egg laying birds that do not have enough calcium available in their diet.
- In the case of chicks you will see that deformities in the bone and joint are very common.
- Spay leg formation is seen in birds that have less calcium intake.

Treatment

Supplementation is the best option when your bird has calcium deficiency. However, you need to be very careful when you are giving these supplements to your birds.

If not done properly, excessive amounts of phosphorous and calcium can lead to other complications.

If the level of calcium is beyond the necessary amount, it can lead to mineralization of the kidney and kidney failure. When calcium is available in large amounts, the absorption of essential trace elements like zinc and manganese is affected.

If the level of phosphorous is too high, it is seen that calcium is not absorbed properly. This is because any calcium in the body will be bound in the form of calcium phosphate that is not soluble. As a result, blood calcium levels will be low.

You need to make sure that you do not provide any unwanted supplements if the natural foods are able to provide your bird with all the nutrients that he requires.

Imbalance in Vitamin D
The main function of Vitamin D is to make sure that calcium metabolism occurs in the body of the bird. Vitamin D can be equally problematic if the levels are either too low or too high.

If the diet of the bird consists of an excessive amount of Vitamin D, it leads to toxicosis which means that the amount of calcium absorbed by the body also increases drastically. In the initial stages, this is not an issue as the kidney is able to excrete the excess calcium out.

But with repetitive calcium excess, the function of the kidney is compromised leading to a reduced rate of glomerular filtration. As a result, kidney stones are formed and can be extremely painful for your birds.

There are several factors such as the form of Vitamin D ingested, the amount of calcium and vitamin A in the diet etc. that determine the chances of toxicosis. The health of the kidney us another major factor.

For example, providing cholecalciferol vitamin D supplements are more toxic than supplements like ergocalciferol. In fact, the former puts the bird at 10 times more risk than the latter.

If your bird is being over-supplemented with vitamin D, there are chances that the kidney gets mineralized along with calcification of the blood. If you have fed your bird toxic amounts of Vitamin D3, you may balance it out by reducing calcium in the diet.

In case your bird has any nutritional imbalance, the best thing to do would be to provide the bird with a diet that is nutritionally adequate. Getting them on homemade food is the best option. Of course, you also have the option of providing them with recommended commercial foods.

Mineral sources like calcium carbonate that can be found in egg or oyster shells are ideal for Finches. You can also give your bird natural sources like milk, yoghurt, cheese, spinach and broccoli. If you are giving your bird eggs, make sure that it is not raw to reduce any risk of salmonellosis.

Deficiency of iodine
A seed based diet is usually responsible for iodine deficiency in the body. Thyroxine, which is responsible for thyroid gland function, is not formed in the body without adequate amounts of iodine.

It is necessary to give your bird iodine supplements if you are keeping them on a seed only diet. This supplement can be added into the food or water of the bird.

Goiter is the result of iodine deficiency. The thyroid gland is present in the area where the trachea branches out into the lungs. This is just above the heart. As a result, when these glands become enlarged, a lot of pressure is applied on the voice box and the trachea. You will notice that birds have great difficulty breathing when they suffer from iodine deficiency for this very reason.

You will notice a wheeze, click or a squeaking sound whenever your bird tries to breathe. You will also notice vomiting in birds that have an iodine deficiency.

Goiter develops very slowly but gets very bad progressively. The larger the thyroid gets, the more obvious the sounds while breathing become. In many cases, the bird needs to exert himself physically and hold his head up in order to breathe.

There is always a chance of secondary bacterial invasion or fungal infection. This condition also leads to weight gain, deposits of fat on the internal organs, compromised feather quality and a lot of other secondary issues.

Although this is a rare deficiency in Finches, you need to be watchful. The treatment of the condition is determined by the severity of deficiency.

Treatment of iodine deficiency

- In case of a mild deficiency, adding iodine supplements in the food or water can help.

- In extreme cases, your bird may have to be hospitalized to receive sodium iodide injections daily until this condition is reversed.

- Preventive measures are important following the treatment in the form of good diet and necessary supplements.

Hemochromatosis

Iron storage disease or hemochromatosis is very common in Finches and is the result of the bird's inability to excrete any excessive iron. This leads to damage in the heart, kidneys and the liver. Blood breakdown and chronic stress can be caused by hemochromatosis.

Several enzymes are not formed when there is an excess of iron in the body. In addition to that it also leads to genetic predisposition of the hatchlings to this condition.

You will notice difficulty in breathing along with a distension of the abdomen. Discolored droppings are common with birds who have hemochromatosis.

Treatment of hemochromatosis

- Long-term phlebotomies, or blood-letting, are carried out on a weekly basis in order to reduce the iron deposits.

- The iron levels in blood serum are constantly monitored to ensure that they do not exceed 150mg.

- A hematocrit or CBC is used to make sure that the bird recovers from these blood-letting sessions.

- A medicine called deferozamine has been used to treat this condition as well.

Dietary management is the best way to prevent this condition in your Zebra Finches. Better diets are available for Finches these days. All you need to do is consult your vet. Bottled water is recommended if your bird has had this condition in the past.

Birds that have not had hemochromatosis and have lived long lives have been given a lot of fresh foods and low amounts of seeds. It is best that you also rely on a balanced diet for your birds to prevent the above mentioned nutritional deficiency.

If you are new to the world of Finches, it is recommended that you follow a diet provided by your vet to the T. As you gain more experience with your birds and do your own research, you can mix up the diet. In any case, remember that supplementation without consultation is always prohibited for your birds if you want to ensure that they stay in the best of their health for the rest of their lives.

b. Bacterial diseases

It is very common for birds to develop bacterial diseases. Most often, inappropriate husbandry is responsible for making the birds develop these conditions. Improper nutrition leads to compromised immunity that makes the birds more susceptible to these infections.

Juvenile birds and neonates are even more susceptible to these conditions. The respiratory tract and the gastrointestinal tract are the first ones to get affected by these bacteria.

There are various strains of bacteria that affect birds out of which strep, staph, citobacter and E.coli are the most common ones. These are the bacteria that are associated with humid areas, dust, old food, seed, grit and water. In some birds natural resistance to these bacteria may be compromised due to reproductive diseases in the parent.

84

Most common symptoms of bacterial infection

- Droppings that are watery and green in color.
- Sneezing
- Rubbing the eyes incessantly
- Swallowing constantly
- Coughing
- Yawning
- Coughing
- Change in voice or loss of voice

Bacterial infections, caused by either ingestion or inhalation, are life threatening if left unattended. The exact type of bacteria needs to be identified before giving the bird any form of treatment. That is when you can treat it perfectly and also prevent it from recurring.

Treatment and precautions for common bacterial diseases

- Antibiotics are administered after the culture test is complete.

- Antibiotic drops are given directly to the bird if he is very ill. You can even inject the antibiotics in these cases.

- If the infection is mild, you can administer the antibiotics through drinking water. You need to make sure that the bird is drinking water when you take this approach.

- All the seed, fruit and grit should be removed from the cage.

- Disinfecting the cage on a regular basis is a must.

- The seeds that you provide must be sterile.

- The bird must never be left out of the cage unsupervised.

- If your bird has not recovered fully, you need to make sure that you do not allow him to wander around the house.

There are several things that you can do in order to accelerate recovery in your bird. You can give the birds Turbo-boosters and also energy supplements.

Special Fvite with sterile seeds can be included as a part of the diet of your bird.

Once your antibiotic treatment is complete, you can give your bird loford and dufoplus in water. You need to make sure that your bird is eating and drinking well. If he is not doing so, your vet may have to force feed him.

Bacterial infections can become very severe in the long run. They will damage the kidney and liver if ignored and the bird becomes susceptible to a lot of illnesses in the future.

It is the responsibility of the owner to understand how a certain disease originated in order to help the bird recover faster. In order to ensure that your bird does not have repetitive episodes of infection, you can get a complete health program from your vet and follow it till your bird is fully recovered.

Paying attention to bacterial infections is very important, as humans can also be affected by certain strains of bacteria. The droppings of the bird can spread bacteria. Children are especially susceptible to infection and must be kept away from a sick bird. One example of a bacterial strain that affects Finches and humans is campylobacter.

Remember that bacterial infections are usually related to the surroundings of the bird. If there is any contamination that enters the mouth of the bird, it will lead to the disorder.

Of course, even the best-kept birds may be susceptible to infections. If this happens, it becomes even more important for you to make sure that you understand the source of the infection and try your best to prevent any more in the future.

Here are a few strains of bacteria and the common sources of infection for each one of them.

E.coli :
- Fluctuation of temperature
- Draught
- Stress
- Contaminated food or old fruit
- Wet areas
- Dirty cages

Strep
- Underlying viral infection
- Cold stress
- Dust
- Poor quality of food
- Stress

Staph
- Mice
- Dust
- Poor seed quality
- Contamination in the air conditioning

Diplococcus
- Stress
- Mice

Citobacter and Pseudomonas
- Poor water conditions
- Poor cage hygiene

Many owners believe in a holistic approach to prevent these infections. You may also try the following after consultation with your vet.

- **Goldensea:** This herb is used for its strong antibiotic property. It is effective against E.coli, staph and strep.

- **Echinacea:** This herb is known for killing several pathogens that cause diseases including protozoa, fungi and bacteria.

- **Licorice root:** This herb is antiviral and antibacterial in nature and is known to be effective against the most powerful strain of bacteria.

Most common bacterial conditions in Finches

In the case of Finches, there are two conditions that you need to be extra cautious about. These birds are genetically predisposed to these conditions and may even be carriers of the condition in some cases.

Chlamydiosis

This is a condition that affects almost all companion birds. It is best that you follow all the federal regulations with respect to testing and quarantining for this condition if you plan to have an aviary or if you plan to breed Finches.

This condition is caused by a type of bacteria called *chlamydia psittaci*. The incubation period of this strain ranges from 3 days to a couple of weeks.

The only concern with this condition is that it is easily transmitted from one bird to another through the feces. The bacteria stays infectious in debris that is organic for more than one month.

Symptoms in birds that are carriers:

- Anorexia
- Nasal and ocular discharge
- Dehydration
- Excessive droppings
- Lack of appetite
- Diarrhea

Symptoms in birds that are clinically ill:
- All of the above
- Monoystosis

- Leukocystosis
- Increase in bile acid level

Diagnosis

Diagnosis of this condition is quite difficult, as the clinical signs are usually mild or absent. The most common methods of diagnosis include:

- Antigen and antibody tests
- Serological tests
- PCR testing
- Cloacal swab analysis

Multiple diagnosis methods must be applied because of the nature of this condition, which is actually quite hard to identify and understand.

Treatments

- Doxycycline is the most common treatment option.
- Dietary calcium must be reduced during this treatment phase.
- Medicated feed may be administered if the condition is too severe.

You need to make sure that you devise a proper treatment plan for this condition as it can be transmitted to people quite easily.

Avian mycobacterosis

This condition is usually caused by different types of bacteria including *Mycobacterium avium, M.intercellulare, M.bovis, M.genovense and M.tuberculosis.*

This condition is progressive and usually affects the gastrointestinal tract of the bird as well as the liver. This condition is hard to diagnose because of the limited number of clinical signs available in the initial stages of infection.

Symptoms of Avian mycobacteriosis
- Weight loss
- Anorexia

- Diarrhea
- Depression

Diagnosis of the condition
- Acid fast staining of the culture
- Biopsy of the intestines, liver and spleen
- PCR testing
- Ultrasound

The difficult part in diagnosis is the fact that these strains of bacteria are very hard to culture. Therefore if the culture test is negative it is not conclusive that the condition does not exist.

The other tests are not as sensitive. The best option is PCR testing of a sample of the bird's feces. In some cases, radiographs have been useful in determining the condition.

If you have an aviary with multiple birds, it is also hard to determine which of the birds is actually infected. If you are able to point out the birds that have the highest risk of being affected, you need to make sure that they are isolated and properly monitored.

Treatment
- Antibiotic treatment for 1 year or more
- Administration of multiple antibiotics
- Examination of your own husbandry practices

If your bird is in the advanced stage of this condition, it is less likely that he or she will be able survive. Although there have been no records of the conditions being passed on from birds to humans, you need to make sure that you take all the necessary precautions, especially if you have an immunity that is weak.

c. Viral diseases
Viral infections in birds can be fatal in most conditions. Makings sure that your birds are checked by a vet on a regular basis is the key to keeping birds away from these diseases. With most viral diseases,

the incubation period is very short and the birds may succumb to the infection overnight.

Here are some of the avian viral diseases that may affect Zebra Finches:

Avian polyomavirus

This condition usually affects birds that are young. Usually adult birds are immune and in case of any infection, will shed the virus in just 90 days. Incubation period for avian polyomavirus is 10 days.

Symptoms of avian polyomavirus infection

In the most typical cases, a healthy juvenile bird that is still not a fledgling will develop crop stasis, lethargy and will die in just 48 hours of the onset of the condition. In rare cases, the following symptoms are recorded:

- Abdominal distention
- Cutaneous hemorrhage
- Feather abnormality

Diagnosis of the condition
- Examination of the cloacal swab
- Blood tests
- Virus neutralizing tests
- Antibody tests
- Necropsy testing of the chicks that have succumbed to the condition.

Prevention of the condition
- Keeping the aviary free from visitors.
- Making sure that new birds are only included in the aviary after 90 days of strict quarantining.
- Making sure that you keep up all the practices of hygiene.
- Stopping breeding for at least six months if the condition is diagnosed in any bird in the aviary.
- Disinfection of the nesting boxes and the aviary.
- Avoid purchasing birds from different sources.
- Avoid purchasing birds that have still not been weaned.

Treatment of the condition

As discussed before, avian polyomavirus has a very short incubation period and the symptoms are rarely seen before the bird succumbs to the infection.

You can opt for a vaccine that is available for younger birds. Making sure that you give birds that are breeding a dose of this vaccine at intervals of two weeks in the off-season in a must.

You must also provide these vaccines to neonates before they are 35 days old. You have the option of a booster shot after about 3 weeks as well. Getting your birds this shot prevents the risk of infection to a large extent.

In general, there is no cure for this condition except preventive measures and supportive care after the condition has been diagnosed.

Gouldian Finch Herpesvirus
This is a rather uncharacterized strain of virus that is known to affect Zebra Finches, Crimson Finches and Red faced waxbills. If you have an aviary with multiple birds, you will observe lesions in birds that are affected. However, some of them may be completely unaffected by the virus.

Symptoms of Finch Herpesvirus
- Listlessness
- Ruffled plumes
- Heavy breathing
- Nasal discharge
- Swelling in the eyelids
- Crusts in the cleft of the eyelid
- Inability to eat

After about 5-10 days of the first signs and symptoms of this viral infection, it has been observed that birds are unable to survive. Post necropsy, it was observed that the birds showed thickening of the fibnoid and discharge in the eyes and nostrils. Besides that, the internal organs seemed normal on all occasions.

Herpes virus is considered an alpha strain of virus because of which the incubation period is very short and the damage caused is quite serious. There is no cure for this condition. All you can do is take preventive measures to make sure that the birds are quarantined properly, given ample food and clean water and are kept in the most hygienic conditions possible.

Avian bornavirus

Infections by avian bornavirus in birds were observed quite recently in birds with the first ever records being made in the 1970s. Since then, several species have been considered susceptible to the condition, including Finches. The first evidence of this condition affecting Finches was observed in Estrildid Finches.

This condition is progressive in a few cases or may develop overnight in others. Mortality rates are high in birds that have been affected by this strain of virus.

After several crop biopsies, it was discovered that affected birds have lesions in the heart, the gastrointestinal tract, the brain, spinal cord, lungs and kidneys. The disease may either be transmitted orally or through the feces. It is highly contagious and can be even more problematic if you have a mixed aviary.

Symptoms of avian bornavirus infections:
- Chronic weight loss
- Increase in appetite followed by excretion of undigested food
- Regurgitation
- Convulsions
- Weakness
- Tremors
- Ataxia or inability to control movements
- Blindness

Diagnosis
- Biopsy of cloacal swabs

- PCR testing

These tests need to be carried out once every week for three straight weeks to determine if the bird is really infected or not. The virus is shed intermittently, which makes it even more necessary for you to have multiple tests as well as differential diagnosis for conditions like toxicosis and foreign body obstruction before the conclusions are derived for infection by the avian bornavirus.

Treatment
- Providing the bird with food that is easy to digest
- Administering medications like celecoxib and meloxicam
- Isolation of infected birds as a method of disease prevention
- Regular PCR tests
- Good hygiene
- Ultraviolet light setting

Poxvirus infection
This is a large DNA virus that usually affects the respiratory tract, the oral cavity and the epithelial cells of the internal organs. It is believed that all birds are susceptible to this condition. In the case of aviary birds or companion birds, this condition can be avoided, as the birds will not be exposed to this virus if proper husbandry practices are followed.

This disease usually affects Parrots and Lovebirds. In case of Zebra Finches, your bird may only be a carrier and may never develop symptoms. However, for those with a mixed aviary, this is also cause for great concern as the disease spreads rapidly.

The infection may be cutaneous or systemic depending upon the strain of virus that has affected your bird, the age of your bird, the health of the bird and the route of exposure.

In the cutaneous form, you will notice that there are wart like growths on parts of the body that are unfeathered, including the area around the eyes and nares, the legs and the beak. Another form, which is the diptheric form, shows similar formations on the larynx, pharynx, tongue and the mucosa. The systemic form is differentiated by the characteristic ruffled appearance of the bird.

Symptoms of poxvirus infection
- Lesions on the eye, ear and oral cavity
- Lethargy
- Troubled or labored breathing
- Difficulty in swallowing
- Partial blindness
- Weight loss
- Skin lesions
- Ruffled appearance

Treatment of poxvirus infection
- Supportive care
- Fluids included in the diet
- Vitamin A supplementation
- Cleaning of the lesions on a daily basis
- Antibiotics
- Ointments for secondary infections
- Assisted feeding
- Mosquito control
- Indoor housing

It is also possible to provide your Zebra Finches with certain vaccinations that will make them immune to certain strains of pox virus.

Avian influenza
Commonly known as bird flu, this is a condition that affects almost all species of birds. Most of the causal strains of virus do not affect human beings. However, it was recently discovered that some strains like the A(H7N9) cause serious infections in humans as well.

This is a condition that commonly affects waterfowl but can even lead to outbreaks on a large scale in an aviary set up. The virus is so potent that it has the ability to even affect other mammals. So if you have other pets at home, you have to be very careful and watchful.

This disease has a very aggressive progression. This means that the disease can spread within a few hours and can lead to death as well.

Symptoms of avian influenza
- High fever
- Diarrhea
- Vomiting
- Coughing
- Abdominal distension
- Decreased egg production
- Inflammation of the trachea
- Congestion
- Hemorrhage
- Edema
- Lack of limb coordination
- Paralysis
- Blood in the nasal and oral discharge
- Greenish color of the droppings

Treatment
- Vaccination is the best option to prevent the disease altogether

This condition can be serious if the strain of virus that affects the bird can affect humans as well. In many states it is a mandate to report the outbreak of avian influenza in your aviary to a regulatory authority. Your avian vet should be able to help you with this.

In most cases, antiviral compounds cannot be administered to the bird unless it is approved by these regulatory authorities. Even the vaccination that is used on your birds needs to be approved by the USDA or by the state veterinarian.

d. Diseases caused by parasites
There are both endo and ectoparasites that can affect Finches. These parasites are mostly found in unhygienic conditions. While they are not always fatal, there are chances that the symptoms only become obvious when the bird is already very unwell. That is the only reason why parasitic infections are a threat to the bird's life. In most cases,

a bird seems completely normal and the symptoms become severe overnight.

Here are a few parasitic infections that zebra Finches are most susceptible to:

Coccidiosis

This condition is caused by a certain parasite that is usually found in the intestinal tract of birds. The disease is transmittable and is passed on through the feces or through interaction. The condition is highly contagious and you will notice several birds being infected immediately after you notice the first case in your aviary.

Symptoms of coccidiosis

- The vent area is wet
- The bird has consistent diarrhea
- The feathers are fluffed up
- The bird has very little energy when you approach him
- The bird tends to sleep a lot

Treatment
- A course of sulfonamide or sulphadim is required
- The cage needs to be cleaned regularly to prevent any sort of infestation in your aviary.
- The drinking containers should be made only from glass or plastic while providing any antibiotics
- You may continue a course of broad spectrum antibiotics.

Parasitic worms
If your bird is being fed any live foods, worms are easily picked up. It is therefore necessary for you to make sure that the live food that you give your bird is fresh.

Another source of parasitic worms is the droppings of birds in the aviary. If the parent bird is a carrier of parasites, they may transfer it to the young while feeding.

When you have an outdoor cage, you need to make sure that there are no droppings of wild birds in your aviary. This is the primary source of several parasites and infectious diseases.

Symptoms of parasitical worms
- Weakness
- Worms are spotted in the feces of birds
- Worms are seen in the water dishes

The disease is fatal only when the condition is not treated properly. The most common worms that affect Finches are threadworms, caecal worms, tapeworms, gapeworms, tapeworms and roundworms.

Treatment:
- Have a routine worm management program for your bird
- A broad spectrum wormer like levamisole can be administered to the bird
- Have your birds tested regularly

Scaly face
This is a condition that is also known as Knemidocoptes jamaiscensis. When mites borrow into the feathers of the bird and lay eggs there, this condition is caused.

The condition gets worse when the eggs that have been laid in the feathers hatch. The most common way of transmission for this condition is when the parent birds feed the young. It has been observed in adult birds as well but the source of transmission is not very well known.

Symptoms of scaly face
- A scaly film is seen on the skin
- The scales may be formed on the eyes if left untreated
- Scales are seen on the legs of the bird

If you ignore this condition it will become fatal, as the scales will slowly spread all over the body. The parasites are demanding and will lead to the death of the host.

Treatment
- Paraffin is administered to birds that have been affected by this condition.

Air sac mites
This is one of the most common conditions that you will see in Zebra Finches. The mite that causes this condition is scientifically called *Sternostoma tracheacolum.*

The condition affects the respiratory system of your bird, leading to a lot of labored breathing. The disease is transmitted during courtship and also when the parents feed their young.

Symptoms of air sac mites
- Coughing
- Loss of voice
- Abnormal chirping
- Labored breathing
- Fatigue

Treatment
- An insecticide is used to eradicate the mites fully.
- A spray containing ivermectin can be used in the cage.
- All birds, including the ones that are not affected should be treated for air sac mites.

These parasites have a life cycle of 6 days before which you need to make sure that your bird is treated. If the eggs hatch before treatment, the process becomes a lot more tedious and the condition progresses rapidly.

e. Accidents and injuries
Birds are always prone to accidents and injuries, especially when they are in an aviary. If you let your birds outside the cage, there are several things that can lead to accidents such as sharp edges of furniture, closed windows or even doors.

If your bird does suffer from an injury when he is moving around the house or if he has a fight with another bird, providing timely first aid is the key to helping your bird recover faster.

Broken wings

Broken wings are a very common injury with birds because of the fragile nature of their bones. With Finches, flight is the only mode of exercise and defense. When the wings of these birds are broken and not set properly, they tend to compromise the flight of the bird forever.

It is best that you take professional assistance if you have no experience with birds. However, providing first aid can relieve a lot of pain. If the wound is accompanied by open cuts or bruises, it is best that you call your vet immediately.

Helping a bird with broken wings

If your bird is stumbling on the floor of the cage and is holding one wing lower than the other, it could be signs of a broken wing. Here are a few things you can do if you suspect that your bird has a broken wing.

- Pick up your bird and put him in a carrier. The bird must be shifted to an area that is quiet and secluded.

- Once the bird has calmed down, check his body for any other injuries. In case of any cuts, you can clean it with an antibacterial solution.

- In case of profuse bleeding, dabbing some cornstarch on the wound can really help the bird.

- Cut a 12inch strip of bandaging tape. This is the best option, as it will not stick to the feather of the bird.

- Pick the bird up and gently hold the wing that is broken against the body of the bird.
- The bandage should be tight enough to hold the wing in place and can be secured under the wing that is intact.

- Let the bird walk around after the wing has been taped. If he is unable to walk or if he is unable to breathe, you may have to adjust the bandage.

- The bandage should be left on for about 4 weeks. You can consult your vet in order to provide the bird with supplements to aid the healing process.

- If the bird is unable to fly even after 4 weeks, he will have to be rehabilitated at a local facility.

Cuts and bruises

There are several causes for bruises and cuts in birds. Usually when a blood feather breaks, it bleeds quite profusely. This is the easiest form of bruise to heal.

Helping a bird with a broken blood feather

- The first thing you need to do is control the bleeding. Styptic powder or flour can help control bleeding.

- If that does not help, hold the wound down with gauze and apply a little pressure. This will keep the bleeding down till you take the bird to a good vet.

- The bleeding shaft is usually pulled out to prevent blood loss. You may do this at home if you have experience with birds. If not, it is best that you take your finch to the vet.

The next most common cause for injury is attacks by cats or dogs. This causes a lot of stress to the bird and you need to be extra cautious when dealing with this sort of injury.

Helping a bird who has been attacked

- Take him to a quiet room and keep him warm. This will help him recover from the shock of being attacked.

- In case the wound is bleeding, you can control it by applying pressure with a piece of gauze. But, be sure that you are not hampering breathing in any way.

- The bird must be taken to the vet immediately in order to avoid any chances of infection. Cat saliva is very toxic for birds.

- You need to check for any broken bones. In case of broken bones or wings, you can wrap them at home and then take the bird to the vet. In case of broken skull or legs, you must never try to clean it up at home.

Burns

A bird can suffer from burns accidentally if they land on a hot stove or if they touch a hot table lamp while flying around the house. It is very important that owners make it a priority to make their home safe for the bird to live in.

However, in case your bird does suffer from burns despite all the precautions, your bird will require first aid.

Helping a bird with scalds

Scalds are caused by hot liquids, chemicals and fire. In case this accident occurs in your home:

- First wash the burn with cold water and flush it for about 15 minutes.

- If it is a third degree burn, you have to rush your bird to the vet. On the way to the vet, you need to cover the affected area with moistened gauze pads.

- Contact lens saline is one of the most effective ways to cool down a burn as long as it is preservative free.

Helping a bird with electric burns

This is very rare in Finches, as they do not have beaks that are strong enough to bite through electric wires. Nevertheless, they may come in contact with exposed live wires that may lead to the burn. Here is what you can do if your bird has an unfortunate accident:

- Do not touch the bird till you get the bird out of contact with the electrical wire. This puts you also at the risk of electrocution. Turn the electrical source off before you do anything.

- Check the breathing of your birds as well as the heartbeat. It is advisable that you learn basic CPR techniques for birds from your vet.

- Call the emergency clinic immediately. When you are taking your bird to the facility, make sure that you keep him in a container that is warm and dark. You can use a plastic bag filled with warm water to give the bird the warmth it requires.

What you must NEVER do in case of burns
- Never apply ice on the burnt area
- Butter, ointment and grease should never be applied.
- If there are any wounds with debris, do not attempt to clean them.
- Blisters should not be popped.
- Never cover a burn with a towel or any material that has fibres that may stick to the wound.
- If the bird is unconscious, do not give him any oral medications or even water.

After the bird has been treated, make sure that you give him all he IV fluids and electrolytes mentioned by the vet on a regular basis. Antibiotics should be provided as required to make sure that your bird heals fast.

Toxicosis

Toxicosis or heavy metal poisoning is very common in birds. This is mostly because birds are easily poisoned by certain heavy metals like lead, zinc and iron that are found in their environment.

Each of the metals affects the birds in a different way but every one of them is equally hazardous to the bird and must be treated immediately.

Today, people are more aware of the potential issues related to metal poisoning. They take a lot more precautions to make sure that their birds are not at the risk of developing any form of toxicosis.

Like humans, birds also contain a moderate amount of zinc and iron in their body. These minerals are present in their food and are actually necessary for metabolism to occur normally. However, when the levels of these minerals increase to an abnormal level, toxicosis occurs.

Lead poisoning is the least common type of heavy metal poisoning today as most of the pet owners take precautions. You also have better quality toys and enclosures that prevent toxicity in birds.

In case the level of iron increases in the body of your bird, it leads to iron storage disease. This leads to excessive iron deposits on the internal organs of the bird. This leads to problems in the liver and can potentially damage the other organs permanently.

Symptoms of toxicosis

- Tremors
- Constant thirst
- Regurgitation of consumed water
- Listlessness
- Fatigue
- Depression
- Lack of coordination in the muscles
- Seizures

Diagnosis of toxicosis
- An X-ray of the gizzard helps identify the type of metal that has affected the bird.
- Blood tests are necessary to detect heavy metal poisoning.
- If you suspect any chances of heavy metal poisoning, it is necessary that you take your bird to the vet immediately.

Treatment
- There are certain organic compounds called chelates that are used to detoxify any poisoning in the bird.

- These agents can be injected directly into the muscles of the bird to make sure that the blood level returns to normal.
- After the bird recovers from the condition, you can provide oral chelating agents.

The speed of recovery depends entirely on the level of poisoning. You can take preventive measures as well:

- Make sure that you remove any material such as the fencing or the perches and cages that may contain lead or iron.

- Stainless steel is the best option to prevent toxicosis in birds.

- When your bird is playing outside the cage, you need to ensure that no heavy metal is available for the bird to consume.

- Keep stained glass, old paints, fishing weights and lead curtains away from the bird's environment.

- You must also make sure that your bird does not come in contact with any soldered parts or areas.

f. Reproductive diseases

There are a few complications that may occur when your birds reach the breeding age. Particularly in the hens, there are several problems related to the formation of the eggs and the laying of eggs that you need to be aware of in order to have a healthy clutch.

Egg yolk peritonitis

This condition leads to the presence of some egg yolk in the coelomic cavity. The egg yolk is one of the best mediums for bacteria to thrive in and is usually caused by a prior bacterial infection.

The response is inflammatory and you will be able to see abdominal distension in birds that deal with this condition. In most cases, diagnosis is only possible after the death of the bird.

There are several other conditions that occur with egg yolk peritonitis including oviduct prolapse, double yolks, internal laying of the egg and internal ovulation.

You need to make sure that you follow the right lighting recommendations for your bird and also provide them with the nutrition that they require in order to lay the eggs successfully.

This condition is very common in birds that are overweight or have erratic periods of ovulation.

Symptoms of egg yolk peritonitis

- Loss of appetite
- Respiratory distress
- Fluffing of feathers
- Loss of voice or vocalization
- Depression
- Weakness
- Swollen vent
- Swollen abdomen
- Ascites

When the bird shows the symptoms, it is usually accompanied by very obvious nesting symptoms. Diagnosis upon the death of the bird reveals that the fluids contain ascites, which are not present in healthy specimens of Finches.

This condition usually ends in the death of the bird and is sudden or very quick in progression.

Chronic egg laying

Birds require certain nesting conditions in order to breed and lay eggs. The factors that contribute the most towards stimulating a bird to lay eggs are:

- Rainfall
- Behavior of the mate
- Availability of food
- Length of the day
- Competition for nesting areas

If the ideal conditions are available, female Finches do not even have to mate with a partner in order to lay the eggs. This leads to a condition known as chronic egg laying, which can lead to other complications such as calcium depletion or hypocalcemia as well as egg binding.

Preventing chronic egg laying
You can make sure that your bird does not lay eggs by making the ideal conditions unavailable. Here are a few things that you can do:

- Allow your bird to sit on the eggs and hatch them. If you take away the eggs as soon as they are laid, she may continue to lay them. It is advised to leave the eggs in the cage until the bird loses interest in them.

- Nesting material should be removed from the cage. Things like paper and small dark places like boxes or sleeping tents should be removed. If your bird is let out of the cage, discourage him from going behind the microwave, under the table etc. where it is dark and cozy. They may even turn this into a nesting area if you do not pay enough attention.

- Keep the lights in the living area of the birds dim. It is good to increase the dark hours to make the bird feel like the days have become shorter. This will turn their breeding hormones off and will make them sleep for longer.

- Food access can be limited. In the wild, birds will never breed unless they have ample food. If your bird has the habit of laying eggs too often, you can reduce the amount of time that food is available. Instead of keeping the food bowl filled all day, you can reduce the time of food availability to 12 hours. If that does not work, you can speak to your vet to give your bird an austerity diet, which is very low in protein. Giving your bird this diet for about 2 weeks will discourage breeding and egg laying.

- Do not encourage any breeding behavior in your birds. Lifting the tail, rubbing the vent etc. should be avoided. Make sure your birds get good exercise and keep them engaged.

- If nothing works, you can give your bird a hormonal injection after consulting your vet.

The one thing that you need to remember when your bird displays excessive egg laying is that it causes a rapid depletion in the nutrients in the body. Consulting your vet to provide your bird with necessary supplements can help prevent secondary health conditions and infections.

Egg binding

This is a very common but potentially hazardous condition for birds. When the female bird is not able to pass the egg through the cloaca, this condition occurs. Sometimes, the egg may be painfully lodged deeper into the reproductive tract. This condition is most common in small sized birds such as Finches. If the egg breaks internally, it may even lead to the death of the bird.

There are several causal factors for egg binding such as:
- Low levels of calcium in the blood
- Limited sunlight
- Unavailability of vitamin D3 in the diet
- Malnutrition
- Lack of exercise
- Small cages that do not permit movement
- Age of the bird
- Prior illness
- Solitary laying of the eggs

Symptoms of egg binding
- Depression
- Straining of the abdomen
- Fluffed feathers
- Loss of appetite
- Abnormal droppings
- Inability to excrete

A bird with egg binding must be taken to a vet immediately. If your vet is able to feel the egg through a regular physical examination, then it is removed easily. In case the egg is deeper in the reproductive tract, an X-ray is necessary to determine the condition.

Treatment
- If you have any doubt that the bird may have egg binding, you could keep her in a warm room. A steam room or even a warm towel can help relax the vent of the bird and aid the passing of the egg.
- A shallow water bath with warm water will help the bird to a large extent.
- Provide the bird with calcium supplementation.
- You may apply a lubricant in order to aid the passing of the egg. Coconut oil can be of great assistance.

This is a condition that can be potentially life threatening. Taking preventive measures is the best way to help your Zebra Finch. You can provide your bird with a regular dose of calcium shots. In case you want to safeguard your bird from this condition, having them spayed is an option. If that is not an option, you can also ensure that the right breeding requirements are not available to the bird.

Your vet should also be able to provide your bird with Lupron shots, which will prevent the breeding hormones from being produced.

3. Finding the perfect avian vet

Birds are extremely different from other pets. The anatomy and the basic requirements of these creatures is very different. So, you need to have a certified avian vet who can help your bird.

Avian vets have a degree in veterinary medicine but have dedicated a large portion of their practice to birds. Every country has an association that vets can register under to stay updated about this science. One such association is the Association of Avian Vets or AAV. You can find all the registered avian vets in your vicinity using their official website which is www.aav.org.

If you are unable to find a good avian vet on this website, you have the option of asking a regular vet for leads. You may also contact Zebra Finch clubs in your city for more information.

When you are choosing an avian vet, here are a few things that you need to look for:

- Staff that is trained to handle birds. They will be comfortable around your birds and will know a little bit about the species as well.

- There should be an emergency facility linked with the clinic in case your bird needs immediate attention. It is best to look for a clinic that even has a pet hospital for in-house patients.

- The vet should have mostly avian patients. If he is only seeing one or two birds in a day, he is most likely not an avian vet. Some of the avian vets also deal with exotic pets like reptiles but will dedicate most of their practice to birds.

- Each examination should be for at least 30 minutes. If the interval between each patient is just about 15 minutes, your bird may not be getting a thorough examination.

- The clinic should be as close to your home as possible. Drives are extremely stressful for pets and should be minimal.

Your avian vet should also be updated with the facilities available for birds. If he is part of the AAV or attends regular seminars about avian medicine, you can be sure that your bird is in great hands.

Conclusion

Zebra Finches are among the most adorable pets that you can have at home. They are extremely adorable and fun to watch. However, you need to make sure that you give them a good home which they can live in for up to 15-18 years. This is the life span of each bird and is therefore the commitment that you need to be ready to make.

If you plan to move, you will have to make arrangements for a foster home or will have to shift your birds to your new home based on the regulations of the new state or country that you plan to take your birds to.

Nevertheless, these birds are ideal for beginners as they are relatively easy to maintain. If you have kids at home, these birds can also help you teach your child things like responsibility and other values.

Thank you for downloading this book. Here is to hoping that all the information that has been provided makes your journey with your beautiful bird easier.

References

Keeping yourself updated about your birds is always a good idea. The Internet is one of the best sources to learn more and more about Zebra Finches and also interact with previous Finch owners to get answers to any particular queries that you may have.

Note: at the time of printing, all the websites below were working. As the internet changes rapidly, some sites might no longer be live when you read this book. That is, of course, out of our control.

Here are a few websites that will certainly be of great assistance to you as your raise your birds:

- www.zebrafinchsociety.org.uk
- www.cuteness.com
- www.induismglance.wordpress.com
- www.seqzfs.org
- www.birdminds.com
- www.petuniversity.com
- www.thriftyfun.com
- www.lafeber.com
- www.studentswithbirds.wordpress.com
- www.trinesty.com
- www.destinyink.com
- www.efinch.com
- www.kijiji.ca
- www.zebrafink.de
- www.zebrafinch-society.org
- www.zbirds.com
- www.australianFinches.com
- www.australianwildlife.org
- www.finchinfo.com
- www.earthsfriends.com
- www.birdchannel.com
- www.blogs.thatpetplace.com
- www.finchaviary.com
- www.ladygouldianfinch.com

- www.beautyofbirds.com
- www.birdsnways.com
- www.board.birdchannel.com
- www.eol.org
- www.gopetsamerica.com
- www.webvet.com
- www.pets4homes.co.uk
- www.beautyofbirds.com
- www.birds.about.com
- www.birdchannel.com
- www.petsuppliesplus.com
- www.animal-world.com
- www.goodbirdinc.com
- www.associationofanimalbehaviorprofessionals.com
- www.pets.thenest.com

Printed in Great Britain
by Amazon

56313875R00068